Freedom from Anxiety in 5 Steps

BY THE SAME AUTHOR

Stop telling me to cheer up: A practical guide for lifting depression

Stop telling me to talk about it: All you need to know to overcome trauma

For more information on Vivienne Emery and her books, courses and training go to

www.vivienneemery.com

Freedom from Anxiety in 5 Steps

The ultimate guide to liberating yourself from
stress and anxiety

Vivienne Emery

Cover design by Scott Gaunt - scottgaunt@hotmail.co.uk

ISBN: 9798691684678

PublishNation
www.publishnation.co.uk

Dedicated to you.

May these five steps empower you to change the way you perceive your anxiety, allowing you to take back control and become the person you know you can be.

The Five Steps Downloads

The five free audios included with this book can be downloaded directly to your computer, tablet or smart phone.

Each time you listen to the audios, it will become easier and easier for you to be absorbed into a natural state of deep relaxation. As you listen to the visualisation download, you will create new pathways in the brain that will recondition your mind and body to respond and react differently to the physical sensations and thoughts that accompany anxiety. Brain scans show that the more you listen, the deeper the new pathways become so that over time you create new habits in the way you think and behave.

WARNING

DO NOT LISTEN TO THE AUDIOS WHILST DRIVING OR OPERATING MACHINERY.

Contents

Introduction

If fear and anxiety have been holding you prisoner in your own body then it is time to set yourself free. In this five-step programme you will discover the techniques that have helped numerous people liberate themselves from the chains of anxiety.

Anxiety acts as your own personal alarm system. It is there to increase your chances of survival; it sends warning signals when you accidently take a wrong turn down a dark alley, and it enables you to move quickly when you need to escape danger. There is no point, therefore, in looking for a way to eliminate anxiety because you wouldn't last five minutes in this world without it. Instead, you need to understand why this useful alarm system has started to malfunction and acquire the tools to restore and repair it so that you can liberate yourself from the fear and panic that has built up in your body.

In this book you will learn how to take back control and reset the dial on this alarm system so that it works *for* you and not *against* you. Step 1 provides you with an in-depth look at what is going on in your body when you are anxious. After working through this step, you will no longer look at anxiety in the same way.

In Step 2 you will discover the three main reasons why your anxiety levels have become so uncomfortably high. People think anxiety just comes out of nowhere but this is simply not true. The sooner you learn how it became so overwhelming, the sooner you can take action to calm your nervous system.

In Step 3 you will experience the benefits of a variety of techniques and audio recordings that are proven to reset your nervous system, shrink the fear centre in the brain, and reprogramme the mind so that it accepts and allows all emotions to be felt in the body instead of trying to suppress them. By regularly using these techniques and listening to the recordings, you can begin to form new pathways in the brain and develop new habits so that you take back control in stressful and anxiety-provoking situations. Not only will you learn how to observe your sensations rather than identifying with them, but you will also create new coping strategies that you can rely on. Simply knowing that you can choose to respond in a different way will reduce your fear of having any future anxiety attacks.

Step 4 will teach you exercises and tools to let go of unwanted thoughts and change your focus so that you instantly change the way you feel. Mastering your thoughts is an important part of liberating yourself from anxiety; however, you need to go through the first three steps before you can do this.

Neuroscience tells us that the emotional brain turns off the thinking brain when we are highly aroused. This explains why so many people feel frustrated when told to challenge their thoughts during an anxiety attack. When we are fearful, the thinking brain goes offline and our thoughts become rigid so the chances of successfully challenging thinking patterns when we are anxious are very low. You therefore need the first three steps to calm your nervous system so that you are able to keep your thinking brain engaged for longer periods of time. Once the thinking brain is on board, you can use the exercises and audio in Step 4 to master and manage your thoughts.

Finally, in Step 5 you will be shown how you can continue to maintain these invaluable changes. You will discover which type of sleep is extremely important for restoring and replenishing the cells and tissues in your body, and which type de-stresses your arousals from the day. There is a bonus audio that you can use to improve the quality of your sleep and to help you fall asleep when anxiety keeps you awake.

You will also learn about the importance of gut health and discover different activities to keep your nervous system flexible, including a fun exercise that only needs ten minutes a day.

This five-step programme came about as a result of my own personal experience of needing to reduce the stress and anxiety that were being held in my body. I needed to take action that moved me away from useless quick fixes, and to find tools and techniques that would calm my nervous system and strengthen my resilience to future stress and worry. At first I noticed subtle changes but then I began to notice a real shift in the way I felt and thought about external stressors in my life. Although it was not possible to control the events and situations around me, I found certainty and confidence in knowing that I had control over how I responded to them.

I took the techniques I had learned into my therapy clinic to use with the many clients that walked through my door frustrated by trying either to numb their anxiety with medication or reduce it by challenging their thoughts. Some were no longer leaving their houses because they were so fearful of what was happening in their bodies. After working with these clients, I devised a five-step programme that proved extremely effective time and time again. Whether the client presented with trauma, panic disorder, OCD, social anxiety or generalised anxiety, they all benefitted from the programme and made drastic and long-lasting changes within weeks rather than months and years.

The aim of *Freedom from Anxiety in Five Steps* is not to simply share information with you; it is a course within a book. You need to take action to make permanent and valuable changes because transformation comes from *doing* not just *learning*.

The audio recordings and exercises have been included to support and guide you every step of the way. They can be used in the privacy of your own home at your own pace because they will fit in easily around your schedule. There are no difficult or demanding tasks, and no previous experience or skill is needed. You can dive straight into these steps confident in the knowledge that this is a no-nonsense programme based on the latest neuroscience. By using these five steps you will build up a skill set that draws on your mind and body's natural resources, which you can then carry around with you at all times.

* PLEASE NOTE: To protect confidentiality, the personal details in the case histories used in this book have been changed.

STEP 1

What is going on in my body?

Drowning in fear

Jack came into my office, sat down and said, 'It came out of nowhere. I just don't get it. I just don't understand.' He was shaking a little and looked nervous.

'Are you feeling anxious at the moment?' I asked.

'Of course, I am! I'm terrified I'll have another panic attack. It was the worst experience of my life.'

Jack, 34, had come to see me because his doctor had diagnosed him with generalised anxiety and panic disorder. For the past four months he had been on sick leave from work and had stopped all his sport and social activities. He was having difficulty thinking straight and felt as though his mind was constantly whirling. It didn't take much for him to feel extremely troubled by minor outside events. He was also waking up in the night feeling anxious, and wasn't really sure what he was feeling anxious about.

He was angry and frustrated because he couldn't understand why he felt so fearful. 'I don't recognise myself. I used to travel far and wide with just my sleeping bag and a toothbrush, whereas now I have to build myself up just to leave the house. Some days, I feel like I'm drowning in fear.'

The first step towards taking back control was to show Jack what was happening in his body when he was feeling anxious, especially on the day of his panic attack. Having had a similar experience myself, I know how reassuring it is to have the symptoms explained. I have often found that once people have this knowledge, the fear of having another anxiety or panic attack is greatly reduced. It is why I start with this step with my clients. Panic attacks can be so awful that having another one becomes the new trigger for people's anxiety. They are so fearful of experiencing another attack that they do anything to avoid it.

The physical sensation of fear during a panic attack is so extreme and so unlike anything you have ever experienced before that the mind has to come up with an explanation for these symptoms. Your brain will lock onto catastrophic ways of thinking and it will come up with an answer such as 'I must be dying'.

Below is a list of statements that people say to themselves whilst enduring a panic attack.

'My heart is going crazy; this can't be normal. I must be having a heart attack.'

'My legs are shaking. I'm going to faint.'

'I can't take in any air. I'm going to suffocate.'

'My stomach feels so unsettled. I don't know whether I need to be sick or go to the toilet. Are people watching me? I don't want to humiliate myself.'

'I feel like I'm outside my body. Am I going mad?'

All the physical sensations we experience during an anxiety or panic attack are perfectly logical when we understand why they are there. The brain believes you are in life-threatening danger and has told the body to turn on your survival response or 'fight-or-flight' response to protect you, so that you can stay and fight or run away from the danger.

If your life was truly in danger and you needed to fight or run away, what would need to happen in your body for you to do this? You would need all the responses that you usually have when taking part in extreme exercise, so your sympathetic nervous system would be activated. This means your blood pressure would increase and your heart rate would accelerate. Adrenalin and other stress hormones would be released. Your breathing would become short and shallow and your blood would be diverted away from the stomach to the major muscle groups so that they are ready for muscular effort.

If you were to put on your sports shoes and hit the gym for an intense workout, the sympathetic nervous system would activate the same physical reactions in your body. An anxiety attack feels terrifying because you are standing still when you should be moving. The intense fear you feel towards this wrongly-timed exercise response is what drives your thoughts, such as 'I must be dying' or 'I must be going mad'.

Let's look again at the common beliefs people have when experiencing a panic attack and see what is really going on in your body and why.

> **1. 'My heart is going crazy; this can't be normal. I must be having a heart attack.'**

It is normal for the heart to beat this quickly when your fight-or-flight response has been triggered. The body is expecting you to run for your life because it thinks you are in danger. It feels unnatural because you are not running or fighting or taking any form of action. Unless you have a heart condition, this accelerated heartbeat is not usually a threat to your heart. If you are worried about your heart, however, it is best to seek medical advice.

> **2. 'My legs are shaking. I'm going to faint.'**

The body rarely faints during a survival emergency because it wants to take action in order to evade danger. The feeling of weakness in your legs is caused by the shaking in your limbs. Your legs are actually stronger than usual because they are preparing to run. They are shaking because you are not running. Your legs are like a revved-up car with the handbrake on.

3. 'I can't take in any air. I'm going to suffocate.'

When the body thinks you need to run away from a dangerous threat, your breathing becomes short and shallow. The body needs to take in oxygen because it is preparing itself to take action. The more you move, the more oxygen you need. If we start to panic instead of taking action then our breath becomes too fast and too shallow. We start to hyperventilate and, as a result, we take in too much oxygen. This is a problem. Too much oxygen is a problem? Yes, because the quicker you breathe oxygen in the quicker you breathe carbon dioxide out.

Oxygen is an extremely sticky molecule. It sticks closely to the red blood cells that carry it around to the tissues in your body. The body needs carbon dioxide to break the bonds that bind the oxygen to the red blood cells. If oxygen can't be released, it stays stuck to the red blood cells and it is breathed out again taking the much-needed carbon dioxide with it. Although you are breathing quickly, you are not receiving any oxygen. You start to feel like you have no air; you begin to panic, try to breathe in even more oxygen and the cycle repeats until you end up hyperventilating.

Only when there is enough carbon dioxide again can the oxygen be released. This is why people tell you to hold your breath or to take slow, deep breaths. All of this sounds like crazy advice when you feel like you are suffocating – 'I'm not going to hold my breath, I can't breathe!' – but it is the quickest way to restore your breathing and to get the much-needed carbon dioxide into your body so that oxygen can be released. It can seem like it is taking forever to restore the levels of carbon dioxide but keep going, otherwise you will continue to panic and start hyperventilating again.

It may also help to know that it is impossible to suffocate this way. You will not run out of oxygen; the worst that can happen is you will pass out and while you are passed out the body will restore balance to your breathing. Hyperventilation is also responsible for a number of other sensations during a panic attack such as chest pains, feeling faint and feeling numb.

4. **'My stomach feels so unsettled. I don't know whether I need to be sick or go to the toilet. Are people watching me? I don't want to humiliate myself.'**

Blood is diverted away from the stomach and towards the limbs so that you can take action. Eating is not a priority and so digestion stops. You may feel the need to vomit or defecate because the body wants to make you lighter to help you run faster. People are generally kind and would come to your aid rather than stand and laugh at you; not many people would laugh at someone who was clearly in distress.

5. **'I feel like I'm outside my body. Am I going mad?'**

A panic attack is utterly terrifying. The sensations you feel are so intense that after a while the body can no longer tolerate this high intensity of sensation. The only way to cope and to protect the mind and body is to go 'offline'; this is known as dissociation. When we dissociate, we feel as if we are in a dream-like state; it can feel like an out-of-body experience. We can also feel numb.

Dissociation is a natural defence mechanism to help you cope with the intensity of your fear and help you lower your state of arousal. It is known as the 'flop' response (we will look at this later on). If you have never felt these sensations before – and many people haven't – it is understandable why you could think you are going mad. You are not going mad; if you were really going mad, you wouldn't be aware of it or be able to question yourself.

It is also useful to know that a panic attack will peak after about ten minutes. The body can't sustain that level of intensity over a long period of time; however, it can take up to an hour or more for the body to recover and calm down. If you were to suddenly do two hundred star jumps without stopping you would also need time to recover, so don't let this recovery time frighten you; it is a natural response.

It is important to get checked out by a doctor, so that other medical conditions can be ruled out as a cause of these symptoms. Once you know they are the result of this survival response, you can remove the fear from these sensations. No matter how strong their intensity, they can't harm or hurt you.

An exercise response at the wrong time and place

We have just looked at how the body reacts when it believes it is in extreme danger. As mentioned above, the majority of these bodily reactions are the same reactions you have when you exert your body during extreme exercise.

The reason you feel terrified during an anxiety attack is because these sensations come on whilst you are standing still in a queue in the supermarket or sitting down on the bus or in your car. You can't understand why you are feeling like this because there doesn't seem to be any logic to it, so you tell yourself there must be a problem. There *is* a problem: you are not doing what the body expects you to be doing. Your brain for some reason (we will look at the reasons later on in Step 2) has told your body there is danger. The body says, 'Oh okay, let's get out of here then.' It sends messages to the heart, lungs, muscles and stress hormones to go, go, go!

The body has done all this to help you. It is expecting you to run or to fight and use up all this great energy juice, and it can't believe you continue to stay immobile. As I mentioned before, you are like a car revved up with the handbrake on. The body is screaming, 'Move!! Let's go!! Take the handbrake off!'

Instead of moving, you get angry with your body and feel confused. You get locked in negative thought patterns about dying, which only fuels this energy response because your thoughts are now confirming that there is a dangerous threat and you are about to die or go mad. The reason your panic attacks last so long is because of your thoughts. If you were to send messages to the body such as 'There is no danger' or 'Calm down', you would lower your arousal. Instead, you start telling the body that you are about to have a heart attack or that you are losing your mind. By telling yourself and your body that there is now real danger and you are dying, the body screams, 'Oh my goodness, then let's really get out of here!' It slams its foot down flat on the accelerator – but you still have the handbrake on!

Having an anxiety attack is such a petrifying experience because the physical sensations are so unbelievably intense. You can start to take back control, however, once you understand what is going on in your body. This gives you a different perspective on what you are feeling and for many people this stops future anxiety attacks from escalating.

Having a logical explanation for any symptom or sensation in our body will often reduce our anxiety. The two examples below illustrate this.

Example 1 – no logical explanation for sensations

Amy woke up yesterday with a pounding headache; it was so intense that it hurt to breathe. She started to feel worried but she got up and went to work. When she was at work, she looked up 'painful headaches' on the internet and started to feel even more anxious. By the time she got home, the headache hadn't eased at all and her anxiety was through the roof. Her worrying thoughts kept her up most of the night.

Example 2 – logical explanation for sensations

Amy woke up yesterday with a pounding headache; it was so intense that it hurt to breathe. She was just starting to feel worried when she remembered she had drunk two bottles of cheap wine the previous night. Her headache continued to scream at her as she got out of bed, but her anxiety faded away. She went to work and struggled to get through the day. Her headache continued to rage, but then she wasn't expecting it to improve anytime soon. When she got home, she crawled into bed and fell asleep.

Knowledge is power. If you have a clear understanding not only of *what* is going on in your body but also *why,* it becomes easier over time to deactivate the alarm bells. When you begin to feel your anxiety coming on you can say, 'Okay, my heart is beating really fast right now and I feel really shaky – that must be my fight-or-flight response kicking in. My body thinks there is a threat and is trying to help me escape.' Instead of fighting your sensations, allow them in and label them. Your body is trying to protect you from danger. Help your body by sending the message that you are safe.

I know this is easier said than done. The techniques and audios in this book will teach you how to do this.

Increase your tolerance towards your sensations

If the normal side effects of doing an energetic workout mimic the physical experience of panic, it would make sense to use gentle exercise to help desensitise ourselves to symptoms of anxiety. Some people feel wary and fearful of the changes that occur in their bodies even during exercise, so it is a good idea to start off with a low-impact workout in order to tolerate a small temporary increase in sensations during and after exercise. An example would be to do a couple of star jumps to notice what bodily changes take place, such as accelerated heartbeat, shallow and rapid breaths, muscle tension, feeling hot. Then, as you rest, be aware of these experiences fading away.

Work up to a long, brisk walk; if possible, in time go for a run. The idea is to slowly become comfortable with a certain amount of discomfort. The audios and techniques in this book will help to retrain the mind so that you start to observe your physical experience rather than get caught up in it. Getting to know your own body and what it is capable of will put you back in control so that you no longer see your symptoms as terrifying but as normal and expected.

*Please note that it is always a good idea to check with your doctor before starting a new exercise regime.

The long breath out technique

When it comes to your body, your breath is in charge; whatever your breath is doing, your body will follow suit. Earlier we saw that when we want to be active or when we are fearful the sympathetic nervous system is activated. Our breath becomes short and shallow, which sends signals to the rest of the body to accelerate the heart rate and release adrenalin, etc. If we have a system that stimulates the body in this way, it makes sense that we also have a system that relaxes the body. We do: we have the parasympathetic nervous system that activates the relaxation response. The quickest way to stimulate this response is to change how we are breathing.

People will advise you to inhale and exhale deeply when you are feeling stressed or anxious. Although this can be helpful, the quickest way to calm your nervous system down is to make your exhale longer than your inhale.

If we were to observe our breath whilst relaxing, we would notice that the out breath is longer than the in breath. Breathing in this way is a sign to the rest of the body that there is no threat and we can remain calm and at rest. When we are stressed or anxious, we can train our bodies to evoke the relaxation response at will by breathing out for longer than we breathe in. This is a basic law of biology and the quickest way to stimulate the relaxation response. If you breathe in this manner, your body will have no choice but to relax. As soon as your breath changes in this way the rest of the body calms down, reducing the speed of your heart and turning off the adrenalin.

Take a moment to try it now. Breathe in for four, then breathe out for eight. In for four and out for eight. Continue to breathe in this way for five to ten minutes. If it helps, play a relaxing song in the background so that the time passes more quickly.

When I spoke to Jack about this breathing technique, he said that he had tried it when he felt anxious but it didn't work. Maybe you have tried it when you have been in an anxious state, but after a minute or so (which can seem like forever when you are anxious) you gave up because it wasn't working.

Your frustration is understandable. It can take a couple of minutes for the relaxation response to kick in. This can seem like an eternity when you are stressed and anxious, and you don't always have the patience to stick with it, especially if you feel as though it isn't working. The best time to try out this technique is NOT when you are anxious but when you are calm.

If a new recruit at a fire station was being trained to drive a fire engine at speed in an emergency, they wouldn't give the fireman the theory and then say, 'Well, good luck on your first shift!' No, they would get the fireman to practise when there was no emergency. He would learn how to drive fast and how to make sharp turns without the pressure of a real fire to get to. He would get to know the fire truck, how fast it can go and how long it takes to slow it down when the brakes are applied. Learning to drive the fire engine when there is no emergency would allow him to build his skills so that, when his first emergency call comes in, he feels capable and prepared.

You need to practise this breathing exercise first when you are calm in order to build your confidence in using this technique. You need to experience at first hand the control you have and how effective this tool can be. When you practise with a relaxed mindset, you are more likely to persevere until you begin to feel the benefits. This will empower you to put it into practice in times when you need it most.

This simple yet powerful technique can be used any time during the day to calm your nervous system. It is natural and free, and only needs a couple of minutes for it to start working. Within five to ten minutes, you will start to feel much calmer. Once you have experienced the control you have to calm down your body, you can never again be overwhelmed with panic. If you have something important coming up, such as a stressful meeting at work or a difficult situation to deal with at home, you can do this breathing before, during and afterwards to stay in control.

The more you use and practise it, the more natural and easy it becomes and the quicker you can activate the relaxation response. When I first started to use this technique it took about ten minutes before I felt much calmer, whereas now I feel the effects within a few minutes.

The more I feel it working, the more confident I feel in using it because I know that it will work if I persevere. A couple of minutes can feel like a long time when you are anxious, but don't give up. It won't take long before you start to feel the relaxation response kicking in.

Breath Practice (Audio 1)

I have made an audio track to guide you through this technique.

Please go to https://www.vivienneemery.com/audio

* Please do not listen to the audio whilst driving or operating heavy machinery.

Abdominal breathing

Once you have got used to the breathing count of 'in for four and out for eight', you can start to look at the way you are breathing. We can breathe in two ways: with our chest, or with our abdomen. Chest breathing produces short, shallow breaths and is used when we are exercising or when there is an emergency and your fight-or-flight response has been activated. We should therefore spend most of our time using the second type of breathing.

If you observe a baby or a young child breathe, you will notice that their chest barely rises; it is their stomach that goes in and out when they breathe. Their shoulders don't move and their chest only raises slightly at the end of the inhale.

Take a moment to look at yourself in the mirror whilst taking a few breaths. What is your body doing? Do your chest and shoulders rise on the in breath? Does your head move backwards? If this is what you observed, don't worry – you are not alone. The majority of us breathe in this way because of the busy pace of our work and home lives. This way of breathing, however, sends signals to the rest of the body that you are not relaxed, even if you are relaxing. If the breath is always in the chest, the body believes it is too dangerous to completely let its guard down, which leads to us feeling anxious and on edge. It also restricts how much oxygen we take in.

It is important to retrain the body to use the abdomen when you breathe. Not only will it calm you down, it will also give you more energy because you will take in almost twice as much oxygen. As a result, your concentration and mental capacity will improve.

To fully stimulate the relaxation response and to have maximum energy, you need to take the breath into your abdomen. Follow the instructions below to practise abdominal breathing.

Abdominal breathing

1. Lie on your back and put your mobile phone or a light book on your stomach.

2. As you breathe in, take the breath into the abdomen so that the mobile phone rises up and then comes back down as you breathe out. Focus your attention on your phone and enjoy taking it on a ride, rising up on the in breath and coming down on the out breath. Repeat this several times to get use to the sensation of breathing into your stomach.

3. Remove the mobile phone and place one hand on your stomach and your other hand on your chest. Breathe into your stomach so that your hand lifts up. Notice that your chest also rises, but only slightly and only after your abdomen has risen. Breathe out. Breathe in again, noticing the stomach rising first and then the chest. Breathe out. Pay attention to your shoulders and make sure they remain immobile.

4. Now try this abdominal breathing whilst counting in for four (stomach rising) and out for eight (stomach lowering). On the exhale, breathe all the way out until the count of eight. Push the stomach back

---

towards the spine to squeeze out all of the air. In for four (stomach rising) and out for eight (stomach lowering)

5. Continue to practise this breathing for at least 10 to 15 minutes.

6. Play Audio 1 again. This time, use abdominal breathing as you breathe in for four and out for eight. You can now do this sitting up if you prefer – you only needed to lie down to notice what your stomach was doing.

If you are not comfortable with the count of four and eight, you can choose your own ratio. As long as the out breath is longer than the in breath, your parasympathetic nervous system (or relaxation response) will be activated. This tool is a gift from nature that you carry with you at all times. Practise this technique so that you have the confidence to use it when you need it most. Changing your breath will put you back in the driving seat because you will immediately start to send signals to the body that you are safe and in control.

However, it can feel strange at first. This is why some clients tell me that breathing techniques make them feel worse.

Sometimes when people suffer from an anxiety disorder, they feel reluctant to try relaxation techniques because it can feel strange to move from an anxious state into a relaxed state. If you are new to breathing exercises, you may feel uncomfortable as your nervous system begins to shift, especially if you have been feeling anxious for a long time.

Learning to relax will enable you to take back control. If it takes you longer to feel the benefits of these techniques, that's okay. Your nervous system may have become conditioned to always being in the stress response. Take your time and go at your own pace but do keep practising because if your body is constantly firing the fight-or-flight response it is probably crying out to stimulate its relaxation response.

There are some people who continue to feel extremely nervous when trying to relax; they feel anxious even when they close their eyes. They may be suffering from a condition called Relaxation-Induced Anxiety. This condition is usually due to some prior trauma, especially a trauma from childhood. As a result, they have learned to stay vigilant about their surroundings. They may also have great difficulty falling asleep and even prefer to sleep with the light on. In order to relax the body, it is a good idea to seek additional support to help process the trauma. We will look at therapy techniques for trauma in Step 2.

The emotional brain versus the thinking brain

Many books and cognitive therapies will tell you to challenge your thoughts and think your way out of your panic attack, but this can be extremely hard when you are highly emotional. During the last three decades, we have learnt so much more about how the brain works. This is largely due to the use of MRI scans. In the 1990s, neuroscientist Joseph LeDoux discovered that the emotional brain (which is housed in the limbic system) receives the information that there is danger present half a second before the thinking brain (which is housed in the neocortex).[1] This occurs because we need to make very basic decisions when we are in danger. If there is a bus coming towards us, we don't want to stand still weighing up whether we need to move or not. The emotional brain makes the snap decision for us to move and we dive out the way before we even think about doing it. We don't want any input from our thinking brain because it would slow us down; even a moment's hesitation could result in death.

At the core of cognitive therapy is the idea that we think first and then feel. However, when we are anxious and fearful the emotional brain has the power to turn off our thinking brain.[2] This means that we feel first and then think when we are highly aroused by anxiety and fear. It is, therefore, very difficult to engage the thinking brain when we are in an anxious state. Although it is true that our thoughts and what we focus on can change how we feel, this can only happen when we are not emotionally aroused.

Many of my clients tell me how frustrated they become with themselves when they have not been able to use the cognitive exercises their doctor or therapist has given them. It is a great relief for them to know that this isn't because of their lack of will power or determination. They simply won't have much success until they calm down their nervous system; only then can the thinking brain come back online. Those that have some success do so because they have been working on challenging their thoughts for years. A much quicker route is to reduce the anxiety in the body first.

Although it is taking time, some therapies are beginning to adapt to these new findings. A few branches of Cognitive Behaviour Therapy (CBT) now incorporate a mindfulness component and are called Mindfulness Based Cognitive Therapy (MBCT). Hopefully many more cognitive therapies will adapt to the new findings because cognitive therapy is definitely part of the answer. It is actually a very important part but can only be highly effective once the thinking brain is engaged. For that to happen, we need to turn down the arousal in the body. It is for this reason that we won't be looking at how to manage your thoughts until Step 4.

Fight, Flight, Freeze or Flop

Have you ever seen nature programmes where a lizard freezes in front of a snake to avoid detection, or a gazelle caught in the jaws of a lion feigns death so that the lion releases it? As soon as they are safe, both the lizard and the gazelle will make a run for it to save themselves from being eaten.

Freezing in this way is a survival response activated by the sympathetic nervous system. This is the same pathway that stimulates your fight-or-flight response. The lizard and the gazelle are able to run again at a moment's notice because, despite being completely still or 'frozen', the full survival response continues to race through their bodies. From the outside they look dead but on the inside their hearts are still racing and the adrenalin is still pumping so that they can escape when they get a chance.

Humans also have this freeze survival response. We can see it during a heated argument: when angry, some people shout and scream (they are in fight mode), whereas others seem to keep still and quiet (they are in freeze mode). This freeze response can be infuriating to the person who is shouting because the person who is motionless and quiet comes across as indifferent. They may be motionless on the outside, but on the inside their heart is racing and their stress hormones are rushing around their body! They are not indifferent, they just believe they have a better chance of getting out alive if they don't react.

The next time you are in an argument, notice how people around you respond. Some will take action and fight back as a way to respond to the stress they are feeling; others will leave the room (flight), and then there are those who don't say a word (freeze). The way we respond to stress not only depends on the situation but also on the way we learned to respond to stress as children.

You may have already heard of fight, flight and freeze because they are often mentioned when talking about stress and anxiety. A fourth response that isn't as widely known or spoken about is the 'flop' or 'fawn' response. This is an extremely ancient survival mechanism that we carry with us from our reptile ancestors. We have learnt a lot about this fourth response thanks to Stephen Porges and his research on polyvagal theory in the 1990s.[3] Polyvagal refers to the many branches of the vagal nerve, an extremely important nerve that is responsible for carrying signals between the brain and the rest of the body.

The flop response is the complete opposite to fight, flight or freeze. Instead of having an energetic exercise response when we are stressed, our system shuts down. The body and mind go offline and we flop.

Why would we need to resort to this type of response? If we cannot use fight, flight or freeze as options to escape a dangerous threat, the flop response is activated. This could apply to a person who is trapped in a burning car, or a prisoner of war who is being tortured, or a child who is being sexually abused by a caregiver; in these situations, the stress on the body is immense. The person is petrified and cannot run or fight back. There is no point in freezing because they see no chance of escaping at any point. There is no hope of a way out.

The body and the mind are overwhelmed with stress and fear. It is not possible to sustain this level of stress response in the body for a prolonged period of time, and the only way the body can protect itself is to completely shut down. The body goes into this survival response in order to slow down the heart and other bodily processes.

Our awareness is also shut down as we start to dissociate; in other words, we drift out of ourselves so that nothing matters, including the events around us. We are often not even aware of the physical pain our body is enduring. Victims of abuse and torture have reported watching themselves going through the ordeal from above as if it were happening to someone else. Although these examples are at the extreme end of flop, it is possible to access the first sensations of this flop state when experiencing a panic attack. It is therefore understandable that you start to worry about going mad when you tip slightly into this very unfamiliar state.

Why are these four survival responses to stress relevant to anxiety disorders?

It is important to know and understand what your body is doing when you are stressed. I have spoken about the four survival responses in their extreme forms. These extremes are obviously at the two ends of a scale: being fully alert and ready to fight, flight or freeze, or being so overwhelmed that you shut down or flop. There is, however, a whole range of levels in between these two extreme responses that we dip into all the time.[4]

Let us imagine that our bodies have a stress dial inside them. At one end is +10, where the body is told to activate the full fight-or-flight response; at the other end is −10, where the body is told to shut down completely and flop. In the middle is 0; at this level the body is told that everything is okay and that it can remain calm and connected to the environment.

Ideally, we should spend as much time as possible at 0 because at this level there is little or no stress in the body. However, it is not possible to live without problems so as soon as we are faced with a stress factor such as a high phone bill, being stuck in traffic or arguing with a loved one, our dial starts to move. It can respond to stress in two ways:

- it can start to move up from 0 to +3 on the scale and, as a result, dip into a low-level fight-or-flight response. You begin to feel on edge and anxious as your heart rate increases and stress hormones are released

- it can move down the scale and dip into a low-level flop response. Instead of feeling anxious, you feel low, demotivated and even depressed.[5]

To demonstrate this, let's look at a day in the life of my friend Tim. He wakes up on a Sunday morning, stretches and feels great that it is still the weekend. He hugs and kisses his wife and goes downstairs to make them both some coffee. His dial is in the middle, at 0. He is in a connective and contented state.

The phone rings. It's unusual for the phone to ring early on a Sunday morning, and his heart starts to pound. He starts to move up the dial into fight-or-flight. He wonders if it is his mum and feels concerned as he answers the phone. It isn't his mum, it's a wrong number and he hangs up.

He goes into the kitchen and is greeted by his dog. He smiles at the dog and his dial turns back down towards 0. Tim's wife joins him in the kitchen and they start discussing a dent in the car door that she noticed yesterday. Tim looks out of the window and sees the huge dent on the side of his car. He doesn't have enough money at the moment to get it fixed. He looks across the road to his neighbour's brand-new car and he thinks about how he has never had a new car in his life. He thinks that he is unlikely to have one in the near future because he is never going to get that raise at work.

Tim starts to disconnect and feel a little low. He tunes out of his wife's chatter and feels rather numb and insignificant. His nervous system is responding to his stress but in the opposite direction. It has begun to turn the dial down towards 'flop'. He suddenly becomes aware of his wife shouting at him, something about him being selfish for never listening. She brings up all the other times this week when apparently he had not been listening.

Tim walks slowly back to bed feeling tired and demotivated. He was planning to go for a run but can no longer be bothered. Twenty minutes later, his wife comes in with a tray; on it is a freshly made cup of coffee, just how he likes it, and a plate of scrambled eggs on toast. She smiles a warm smile and says, 'What's up? You look a bit glum.' She switches on their favourite TV series and they snuggle up to watch it. Tim looks at his wife and feels so grateful to have her in his life. His dial starts to go back up towards zero.

I'm sure most people can relate to this scenario of feeling these different emotions within a short space of time and often in one day. Our nervous system encourages it; it is important to be able to move up and down this scale easily because we feel mentally balanced when we can move up and down these levels. A flexible nervous system is a healthy nervous system. Problems arise when we get stuck.

If your dial gets stuck higher than the baseline of 0, you can start to feel anxious most of the time. If it gets stuck below the baseline, you can feel low and demotivated.

If you are suffering from an anxiety disorder, it is possible that your stress dial has been turned up high for too long and it has got stuck. Your feelings of anxiety do not mean you are abnormal; you have just got your stress dial caught in the fight-or-flight zone. The audios, techniques and exercises in this book are designed to help you shift out of this survival response and back to a baseline level.

Jack's reaction

After I had explained to Jack what was going on in his body, he was less fearful of his panic and anxiety flaring up. The knowledge that he was having an extreme exercise response at the wrong time and place gave him the confidence to face future attacks. However, this information didn't stop him feeling anxious in general and he wanted to know where his anxiety had come from.

The next step in helping Jack was to find out why his stress dial had become stuck in fight-or-flight mode in the first place.

Step 1 takeaways

1. Start to take back control by understanding your physical sensations during a panic attack.

2. You will no longer fear you are dying once you realise your body has activated your fight-or-flight response.

3. The fight-or-flight response activates the same bodily sensations you need for exercise: adrenalin is released; heartbeat accelerates; breath becomes short and shallow, and your blood is diverted away from the stomach towards the major muscle groups.

4. Your extreme fear during a panic attack can push you into a low-level flop response. This out-of-body experience (known as dissociation) can cause you to doubt your sanity. You are not going mad; it is a natural survival response to calm down the body because it can't sustain this level of fear.

5. The emotional brain has the power to switch off your thinking brain when you are extremely anxious. Calm your nervous system down first before trying to challenge your thoughts.

6. Use the long breath out exercise to stimulate your relaxation response.

7. Retrain the body to breathe using the abdomen rather than the chest.

8. We need to have a flexible nervous system. Anxiety can become our default setting if our stress dial gets stuck in the fight-or-flight zone.

STEP 2

Where did my anxiety disorder come from?

Normal stress levels

Although we live in a modern world, we are still using an ancient fight-or-flight survival tool that evolved hundreds of thousands of years ago to keep us out of harm's way. We saw in Step 1 how this fight-or-flight response is responsible for turning on the sensations we feel when we are fearful and anxious.

Most people want to know how they can get rid of their fear and anxiety. Any book, course or medication that promises to 'end your anxiety' is not to be trusted because we can't eliminate anxiety, nor would we want to. We wouldn't last five minutes without this fear response; it alerts us to danger in our environment, and it protects us by preparing the body to make instant decisions and to act quickly.

This fear response is not usually a problem when used for its true purpose. I gave the example earlier that, when we see a bus coming towards us, the brain senses danger and prepares the body to take action. Adrenalin is released, the breath becomes short and shallow, and our heart rate accelerates. Once we have jumped out of the way, the body can calm back down again. This survival response only stresses the body for a short period of time and is known as *acute stress*.

Abnormal stress levels

Back in the day, our ancestors would have experienced this acute stress response when face to face with a wild animal or a member of another tribe. Once they were safe and back in their cave, this fight-or-flight response would switch off. Consequently, they had many chances in between these acute stress responses to rest and restore their bodies.

In today's world, however, in addition to acute stress we also suffer from chronic stress. Chronic stress is ongoing stress that occurs when you have constant pressure or worry. Your fight-or-flight response is constantly going off with no, or very little, time to rest and recover in between. To illustrate this, let's go back to my friend Tim to see what an average morning of chronic stress looks like.

Tim isn't woken up naturally and easily by the sun but by the shriek of an alarm clock that sends his body into a mild panic. He picks up his phone and sees an email from work he wishes he hadn't seen. He turns on the radio and feels alarmed by the spread of a new disease around the world. He walks to the kitchen and instantly feels annoyed because a neighbour has parked behind his car and he will have to knock on their door and ask them to move it.

He rushes to pour himself some coffee and spills some of it on the floor. As he is cleaning it up, his wife enters the kitchen and shouts at him for using the wrong cloth; he should be using the floorcloth, not the dishcloth. She tells him once again how clueless he is. Tim's stress levels are sky high and he hasn't even left the house yet.

He gets in the car and starts his journey to work. He is late leaving because he had to wait for his neighbour to move his car and he is now stuck in the rush-hour traffic. To make matters worse, someone has just cut in front of him and Tim didn't manage to get through the lights before they changed back to red.

His day at work is so full on that he doesn't have time to stop for a proper lunch and, at the end of the day, he not only has the long stressful drive home but he also needs to stop off at the supermarket. When he finally gets home, he spends what little evening he has left catching up on a few work emails. After dinner he gets into bed tired and in need of sleep, but two hours later he is still wide awake because he has been thinking and worrying about an important meeting that is coming up. He looks at the clock and feels even more stressed because it will soon be time to get up and he hasn't had any sleep.

Now you might say, 'But these are not big life threats.' No, they are not, but the body responds to stress as if you are in danger and switches on your fight-or-flight response. Although they may be low intensity responses, they all add up. This fear or stress response switches off systems in your body that are not essential for your immediate survival. This means that your digestion, sex drive and immune function get put on hold whilst you are in the fight-or-flight response. If you are constantly firing this response by being stressed all day, day after day, then your digestion, sex drive and immune function can be suppressed long term.

Chronic stress also puts an unnecessary strain on our adrenal glands and, as a result, nasty toxins are constantly being moved around the body. Stress can lead to a whole host of illnesses, such as anxiety, depression, insomnia, headaches, back pain, digestive issues, high blood pressure and heart conditions. An estimated 75% to 90% of all visits to the doctor are for stress-related issues.

No one is immune from stress, and these days there are many external stresses such as work, family life, financial obligations, the news, an inbox full of emails and countless other demands that are put on us. As well as these external threats, we also have internal threats, such as when we run fearful scenarios through our mind. The body senses danger when you worry about these thoughts and it activates your fight-or-flight response.

This ancient survival mechanism is not supposed to be firing all day. We saw in Step 1 that if our stress dial is turned up again and again, it can get stuck there. This prolonged state of stress in our bodies can lead to a constant feeling of anxiety and panic. Anxiety is a message to the body and brain that you are stressed.

Follow your own natural rhythms

Every 90 minutes or so, the body slows down in order to relax and replenish its energy. We can often feel when this is happening because we start to lose our focus or we start to daydream. Instead of helping the body rest and restore, we usually grab a cup of coffee, text someone or just power on through, ignoring our body's need to stop for a short while. The more you continue to override the body's need to rest and replenish, the more your stress dial will stay turned up.

If I were to map out on a line graph what an average day of stress and recovery should look like, it would have high peaks of red (where the person experienced some stress) followed by short green spikes (where their body had a chance to rest and recover). This pattern would be evident across the whole graph: a burst of high red followed by short peaks of green, a burst of red and then a burst of green, red then green.

Take a moment to think about your day yesterday. Did you have any green periods after feeling stressed, or would your graph be a mass of red spikes without any green? Don't forget that worrisome thoughts are also represented by angry red spikes.

My anxiety came out of nowhere

It may feel that way but it isn't the case. If your day is full of red stress spikes with few, if any, green spikes then your body starts to have the fight-or-flight response turned on all day. There is a severe cost to the health of your nervous system as a result, and over time this chronic stress starts to adjust your natural level for stress tolerance. As I mentioned above, your stress dial is now permanently turned up high so it doesn't take much for you to feel nervous and on edge. It also doesn't take much to push you into a full-blown panic attack.

You can then start to experience symptoms of anxiety all the time. You feel shaky, agitated and restless. You have a rapid heartbeat and there are uncomfortable sensations in your stomach. You begin to have a general feeling of fear, and falling asleep becomes increasingly difficult.

There may be times when the anxiety is extremely high and other times when it is just simmering in the background but still ready to move into a full panic response at a moment's notice. You get caught in a loop of feeling not too anxious and then really anxious and then not too anxious again. Your anxiety starts to increase because you start to fear the feelings that come with being highly anxious. You have fear of fear itself, and your stress dial gets well and truly stuck.

At this point you may seek medical advice and be told that you have an anxiety or panic disorder and be prescribed medication to numb these sensations. Although this medication can bring great relief to many people, it only treats the symptoms and not the cause. The volume on your sensations may have been turned down, but the song is still playing. You need to treat the cause by resetting your stress dial and shifting your body out of the fight-or-flight setting.

How can I help my mind and body rest and restore during the day?

When someone decides to get fit and healthy, they don't eat one bowl of salad and then say, 'Great, now I will be in good health for the rest of my life.' In order to make permanent changes, they need to commit to a new lifestyle of eating a balanced diet and taking regular exercise.

The same principle applies when resetting your nervous system. There is no point in looking for a quick solution because your anxiety will continue to yo-yo up and down without any permanent changes being made. Don't try the audios and techniques in this book once as a quick fix. It is important to commit to using them as often as you can in order to bring your anxiety levels down permanently and to recondition your response to stress. Over time, new patterns will be formed and your resilience to stress will be strengthened. The aim of these five steps is not to eradicate anxiety because this is not possible; the aim is to change the way you respond to stress and to adopt healthy habits to keep your stress dial at a base level.

Many years ago, whilst on a yoga retreat, I had a consultation with an Ayurvedic doctor. After my assessment, this doctor told me that my mind was a hundred steps ahead of my body; although my body was working hard to keep the same pace, there would come a day when it would simply give up. I considered all the different ways I could change and take time to reduce the stress in my life, but I continued with my previous routine as soon as I got home. Then, about three years later, I was diagnosed with an autoimmune disease. It was a breakthrough moment for me. I started to look into ways of destressing my body without having to radically change my lifestyle.

The aim of this book is not to drastically change the way you live your life. I know first hand how difficult it is to have a new regime and stick to it. It is not my intention to tell you to sit in a cave and meditate all day to lower your stress and anxiety levels. Instead, I am suggesting you do a little house cleaning during the day to keep your piles of stress relatively low.

I have created short audios and exercises that you can do during the day to increase the number of calm green-spike periods in between those stressful red-spike periods. A few small changes here and there can have a big impact on your nervous system and your mental well-being. I have spent a long time studying different techniques and practices that deeply relax and restore the body; the ones I recommend in this book are the ones I continue to use in my own life and in my therapy because time and time again they show great results.

You could schedule in your diary when you will take five-minute breaks during the day, or you could follow your body's natural rhythms. I mentioned above that every 90 minutes the body slows down to rest and replenish; you can learn to tune into these moments and instead of overriding them you could close your eyes and use one of the short audios. After a while you will be able to do these techniques without listening to a recording. This means you can do it anytime, anywhere.

In addition to using the audio in Step 1 to rest and calm the mind and body, you can do an exercise where you count your breaths. Not only will it calm your nervous system and give it a much-needed break, but over time this technique will also improve your concentration in general, enabling you to stay focussed on work or home tasks for longer.

Try the following exercise.

Counting technique

1. Settle into a comfortable position with your eyes open or closed.

---

2. Use your abdomen to breathe in and out deeply.

3. Start to count your breaths from one to twenty (not out loud, but in your mind) like this: inhaling one, exhaling one; inhaling two, exhaling two, and so on at your own pace and rhythm.

4. The idea is to stay with the breaths and the numbers but you will find (sometimes very quickly) that your mind gets distracted by other thoughts. When you recognise that this has happened, gently bring your attention back to counting your breaths. Don't worry if you don't get very far because this is normal, especially if this is new for you. The aim is not to get to twenty every time but to reduce the time it takes to realise you have got caught up in another thought. There should be no judgement, just curiosity at how hectic your mind is at that moment.

The more you practise, the less time it will take you to realise you have lost your concentration. This technique calms the nervous system and the mind; it also trains the mind to remain undistracted for longer periods of time.

As well as using this technique during the day, I also use it at night when my racing thoughts prevent me from falling asleep.

Guided Imagery and Breath Counting Practice (Audio 2)

We can use guided imagery to shift the mind and body from a stressed state to a relaxed state because seeing yourself in a calm and relaxing place sends signals to the body that you are not in any danger. Even a few minutes can refresh and recharge you because it allows your body and mind to sink into a deep state of relaxation. I have therefore combined the counting breath exercise with a guided imagery exercise.

Please go to https://www.vivienneemery.com/audio

* Please do not listen to the audio whilst driving or operating heavy machinery.

So far in Step 2, we have looked at how chronic stress activates our fight-or-flight response so that your body and mind are constantly receiving signals that you are not safe and need to be alert and ready to take action. Being in this state means your heart rate is faster than normal, your breathing is short and shallow, you feel shaky and your stomach feels unsettled. If there are no opportunities to rest and restore your system during the day, the stress builds up and your dial can become stuck in this survival response. Not only do you begin to feel anxious and on edge most of the time, but it doesn't take much to push you up even higher into a panic attack. Anxiety could therefore be a result of chronic stress. There are other factors to consider, however, so let's now look at another possible cause.

Traumatic memories

In general, Jack didn't think that his work or home life were overly stressful. When he looked back on his life, he told me that he had always felt anxious even as a child. I asked Jack to tell me more about his experiences whilst growing up. He told me that his mother had died at home whilst giving birth to his younger brother. He said he was seven when it happened and that he would prefer not to talk about it because he didn't like to think about that time in his life. Although I didn't push Jack for any details, I did ask him to tell me how strong his physical sensations were when he thought about this period. I gave him a scale of 1 to 10, where 1 was low physical arousal and 10 was extremely high. He told me it still felt as though it had happened yesterday and it felt like a 10.

After a traumatic experience 75% of people will, in time, be able to label this terrible incident as a 'past narrative event'. It will always be a difficult and painful memory but it will no longer produce the same traumatic sensations as it did at the time. However, 25% of people will hold on to this memory with all its emotional content. People can carry round a memory like this for more than fifty years and still feel like it happened only yesterday.

In order to remove the emotion from the memory, the brain needs to see it as an event that happened in the past. The brain can only do this when it is calm and relaxed. For some people who have been traumatised, the mind and body cannot calm down long enough for the memory to be labelled as a past event. The emotion around the event remains so high that the memory stays in the highly emotional part of our brain, a structure known as the amygdala. Emotional memories that are held in the amygdala remain active and live. This part of the brain lives only in the present. If a traumatic memory gets stuck there, it will feel live and present even if it happened many years ago.

The traumatic event has passed but the unconscious mind and body don't know that. The person remains hypervigilant and fearful. When this memory is triggered, it produces the same emotions and reactions as if the event is happening in the present moment. This explains the awful symptoms many people experience when suffering from PTSD, such as high anxiety, flashbacks, panic attacks and intrusive memories. Their nervous system is stuck in the fight-or-flight survival response.

Although it is beneficial to talk about difficult experiences and events in our lives, when people are severely traumatised the area in the brain responsible for producing language (Broca's area) shuts down. Some children who experience trauma are unable to talk after a traumatic event for months or even years. Asking a traumatised person to recount their experience can be very challenging and it can embed the trauma even further. Before the client can start talking therapy or cognitive therapy, they need to remove the emotion that is attached to the traumatic event.

Trauma treatments such as EMDR (Eye Movement Desensitisation and Reprocessing) and EFT (Emotional Freedom Technique) can be effective in reducing the strong emotion in the client so that the memory can be processed. Although I have helped a number of clients by using these techniques, I have had the most success with a technique known as the Rewind technique. Often one session is all that is needed to unhook the emotion from the memory. The therapist uses guided imagery so that the client remains deeply relaxed throughout the process. By remaining calm, a part of the brain called the hippocampus can stay online and process the memory. It is this part of the brain that gives our memories context. The memory is labelled as a past narrative event and is moved out of the amygdala. As well as being safe, quick and painless, this technique also has the advantage of being non-voyeuristic. The process can be completed without the client needing to tell the therapist intimate details. Once the emotion has been unhooked from the memory, the client can then talk about their experience.

The Rewind technique was first created and used by Milton Erickson, a renowned American psychiatrist and hypnotherapist. It was later developed by Richard Bandler, co-creator of Neuro-linguistic Programming (NLP). Dr David Muss developed it further and called it the Rewind technique so that it could be used when treating PTSD. In 2004, Joe Griffin and Ivan Tyrell founders of the Human Givens Institute refined it even further. [6a]

If you feel you are still suffering from the effects of a traumatic event as a child or as an adult, seek help from a trauma therapist or a therapist who is trained in this technique. All Human Givens therapists receive this training. Due to its high success rate in reducing the symptoms of trauma, this technique is currently the main treatment used by a number of PTSD charities in the UK. [6b]

You can read more about this technique in the e-book *Stop telling me to talk about it*. You can download this e-book for free when you go to www.vivienneemery.com.

Phobias

The Rewind technique also works extremely well to remove fear and anxiety from any phobias that you may be suffering from. A phobia is an extreme irrational fear to a stimulus. If someone has a phobia of worms, there is no point in trying to convince them that worms are harmless because they know that; their fear is illogical, after all. Telling this person to challenge their thoughts and repeat affirmations, such as 'I am not afraid of worms', 'Worms are my friends', 'Worms are good for my garden', are only effective up to the point when they come face to face with a worm. Then their thinking brain goes offline as their emotional brain takes over and, despite how good this worm is for their garden, they have started beating its head to a pulp with a spade before they even realise they are doing it.

We saw in Step 1 that the emotional brain is in control when you are aroused by fear. Challenging your thoughts in these situations can take a very long time and often proves ineffective. You do not need years to overcome a phobia; the Rewind technique can unhook the emotion in as little as one session.

Jack's trauma

After using the Rewind technique with Jack, his arousal when thinking about the day his mother died came down from 10 to a 2. He could now talk about what had happened and what he had seen that day. We were also able to draw a possible link between this traumatic event and the conversations he had been having with his girlfriend two weeks prior to his panic attack. His girlfriend had brought up the idea of starting their own family. Although Jack was open to the idea, it was possible that his trauma had been triggered in his unconscious mind and his stress dial was turned all the way up. It didn't take much on the day of his panic attack to push him over the edge.

Although taking the emotion out of this traumatic memory had a positive knock-on effect on Jack's ability to sleep and his anxiety levels in general, I advised him to continue to use the audios and techniques in order to keep his nervous system flexible and to build his resilience to stress, especially as he had been stuck in the fight-or-flight setting for a long period of time.

We have now looked at two possible causes for anxiety: long-term chronic stress, and trauma. Both of these have detrimental effects on your nervous system and can cause symptoms of anxiety. Anxiety, as already mentioned, is a message to the body that you are stressed. We can be stressed due to our lifestyle or due to trauma that is still being held in the body and keeping us on high alert. Let's now look at a third possible reason for anxiety.

Anxiety is a signal to the mind and body that we are not meeting our innate emotional needs

If you wanted a stress-free life, you could set up home in a cave and never come out. However, although this way of living would eliminate all your external stresses, it wouldn't put an end to your feelings of anxiety. This is because we are born with an innate programme to meet our physical and psychological needs and our bodies feel stress if we fail to meet them. For example, when we skip a meal the body sends us a message of distress, which is received as a feeling of hunger. If we continue to ignore this message and don't eat anything for the whole day, the messages from the body to the brain become very intense. The body is no longer asking you to eat something, it starts screaming at you to find food. This is why severe hunger pangs are extremely painful. This hunger message puts stress on the body; only when you eat something to meet this need does the stress ease and the message stop.

As well as having an innate drive to meet physiological needs, we are born with a template to meet psychological needs (also known as emotional needs). Many areas of psychology now focus on the importance of meeting these. Psychologists have found that if you are meeting these needs in a balanced way, you are far less likely to experience problems such as anxiety, depression, alcohol or substance abuse because you are more likely to feel happy and fulfilled.[7]

Different schools of psychology divide and categorise these emotional needs in a variety of ways. Some schools group the needs into three main groups, whereas others have divided them up into twenty.[8] For ease of understanding, I have divided them into six main categories.

The six emotional needs below are innate in all of us, no matter our background or culture. They need to be met in a balanced way in order to have good mental health. When these needs are not met in a balanced way, the body feels stressed and sends a message to the brain. This time the message doesn't come in the form of hunger but in the form of anxiety.

If you feel anxious and you don't know why, it could be because you are not meeting one or more of your emotional needs. Your anxiety will continue until you meet this need, just as you will have the message of hunger until you eat something. A lot of mental ill health is a result of failing to meet emotional needs.[8]

The six emotional needs

We all have a need to:

Feel safe and secure

Feel in control of our lives

Feel significant and that we matter

Feel loved and connected to others

Feel we have meaning and purpose in life

Feel we are contributing to others

For good mental and physical health, you not only need to meet your needs but you also need to meet them in a balanced way. For example, if we were to eat too much, we would feel sick and uncomfortable. This is a message that we have overly met this physical need.

Let's take a look at our emotional needs now and see why it is important to meet them in a balanced way.

A need to feel safe and secure

We need to feel safe and secure in all major areas of our life. If we don't feel secure in our job, in our relationships or in our home, we can feel very anxious. If we have gone through a traumatic event, we may try to over meet this need for safety by staying home all the time.

A need to feel we have control over our lives

We need to feel we are in charge of our destiny and the choices we make. If you become seriously ill, or if you are being bullied at work or in a relationship, you will feel a loss of control. If you are someone who tries to have too much control over your life or over other people, you risk having a life that is predictable. A lack of variety and uncertainty can cause stress and anxiety because the mind and the body feel bored.

A need to feel significant and that we matter

We need to feel respected in the roles we have in life, whether it is as a friend, a parent, a partner, or an employee. We need to feel rewarded and appreciated. If you believe you don't matter or that you are inferior to others you can feel very anxious. Often people will join a gang in order to feel respected and accepted, especially if they are not receiving this attention in their own home. People can over meet this need by turning to violence because having power over others can offer a feeling of status and significance.

A need to feel loved and connected to others

There is lots of evidence to show how important it is to give and receive love and attention. For example, it was reported that new-born babies in an orphanage who were fed but not touched or given any eye contact died within four months. The babies that received some (but minimal) attention grew up with severe behavioural issues.[9]

Loneliness is considered to be a bigger killer than obesity, and many links continue to be found between loneliness and ill health.[10] When we feel alone, danger signals are sent out to our bodies because we evolved to be part of a group. We don't have sharp teeth or claws, so the best chance our ancestors had of survival was to be part of a tribe. We may now be living in a modern and relatively safe world, but when we feel alone our two-million-year-old brain constantly feels anxious and on edge.

You don't have to be part of a big tribe; just knowing that there is one person in your life who has your back no matter what is enough. However, avoid over meeting this need by spending 24/7 with this person because it is also important to have privacy and time to yourself.

It is useful to note here how group disapproval can cause a lot of anxiety. Our ancestors were terrified of being thrown out of the tribe because they wouldn't have lasted five minutes on their own in the wild. Our brains are still wired to think this way, and that can help to explain why more and more links are being made between anxiety and the use of social media.[11] Not only do we constantly compare ourselves to others, we worry about how others perceive us. We agonise over why no one has liked our post or why we haven't received a message that everyone else in the group received. If you find that being on social media is causing you a lot of distress, consider cutting down on the amount of time you use it.

A need to feel we have meaning and a purpose in life

Our brains are problem-solving machines and never stop wanting to stretch and grow. If you feel stuck, dead or numb inside, it is because you have stopped challenging yourself. The brain rewards us with happy chemicals every time we solve a problem or attain a goal because it wants us to keep going and move on to the next one.

Sometimes anxiety is a message to move, to get out there and try something new. People dream of retiring at a young age and sitting on a beach for the rest of their lives. If you didn't have a brain, you would indeed be very content but, after about two weeks – three at the most – the brain would start sending you messages: 'Is this all there is? Go and do something.' You don't have to work, but you do need to take on new challenges that are meaningful to you.

However, if you spend more time on your goals than you do with your loved ones, you risk over meeting this need. Try to always meet your needs in a balanced way.

A need to feel we are contributing to others

We evolved to contribute to the tribe and we therefore have an innate need to serve others. When we do something nice for other people – loved ones or strangers – we feel a wave of pleasure everywhere in the brain and body because feel-good chemicals are released. True happiness comes from helping others; the quickest way out of feeling anxious or depressed is to shift the focus off ourselves and on to other people. Be careful, however, not to over meet this need by only focussing on others; you also need to take time to care for and look after yourself.

All human beings are wired to meet their innate psychological needs because they are built into the nervous system. Constant anxiety is often a message to the mind and body that we are not meeting one or more of our emotional needs. It is no wonder that the COVID-19 pandemic caused a massive increase in stress and anxiety in many populations.[12] The lockdown in particular prevented us from meeting many of our needs. We no longer felt safe in our home towns. We had little control over what would happen and when. Many people lost their jobs and therefore their purpose. Being isolated meant we could no longer contribute to others, and those who were living on their own couldn't meet their need for face-to-face love and attention.

Step 2 takeaways

1. Anxiety disorders can develop for one or more of the following reasons: 1. Chronic stress; 2. Past trauma; 3. Failing to meet our emotional needs.

2. Acute stress occurs when we are in a life-and-death situation. A full fight-or-flight response is activated and then fades away without much harm being done to the body.

3. Chronic stress is a result of low-level fight-or-flight responses being constantly activated throughout the day.

4. We need to take time out during the day to rest and restore. If we only have red, angry spikes in our day, stress builds up and our physical and mental health are affected.

5. Anxiety is a message to the mind and body that we are stressed and stuck in the fight-or-flight zone.

6. Memories of traumatic events at any stage in our life can stay in our emotional brain. The body believes the threat is still present and live, and keeps us in fight-or-flight mode in order to try and protect us. The body is unable to relax and we feel anxious and on edge most of the time.

7. As well as having to meet our physical needs, we also have to meet our emotional needs. For example, we need to feel safe in our work, in our home, in our relationships and in our bodies, otherwise messages and signals in the form of anxiety are sent to the body and the brain. Not being able to meet our emotional needs has a detrimental effect on our mental well-being.

STEP 3

How can I reset my nervous system?

Tried and tested techniques

Guided relaxation and guided visualisation are now being used in different therapy settings because they have been shown time and time again to be effective in reducing stress and anxiety.[13] In Step 1, I mentioned how important MRI scans have been in helping us learn more about the brain than we have ever known before. They have shown that, with continued use, guided relaxation techniques can shrink the amygdala (a part of the emotional brain which houses the fight-or-flight centre). These scans have also shown us that the brain can change and form new pathways because it is neuroplastic.

I started studying different relaxation techniques in order to reduce my own stress levels. I have experienced first hand not only my nervous system shift out of fight-or-flight, but also an increase in my resilience in handling stress and anxiety. I still use relaxation techniques daily because I continue to feel the benefits and want to keep my stress dial at a baseline level.

These techniques are now a big part of the therapy I use with my clients. When they commit to using the audios and exercises at home in between sessions, they soon begin to recondition their brain and body in how they respond to stress and anxiety. As a result, these clients don't need to be in therapy for months or years. The average length of time I spend with a client is six to eight weeks, even when they present with extreme symptoms of trauma and panic disorder.

An ancient practice that has been found to effectively relieve symptoms of stress and anxiety is called 'yoga nidra'.[14] The first time I used this technique, I felt such a release of tension everywhere in my body that it showed me just how long my body had been starved of deep relaxation.

Yoga nidra is often referred to as 'yogic sleep'. It is a meditation that uses guided relaxation to allow you to enter a state of consciousness between waking and sleeping. It originated in India, and has now spread worldwide. A new form of yoga nidra, known as Integrative Restoration was developed by Dr Richard Miller and is currently being applied by the US army to assist soldiers recover from post-traumatic stress disorder (PTSD). It has been shown to greatly reduce anxiety, trauma, insomnia, and chronic pain.[15]

One of the most effective tools used in yoga nidra is the technique of welcoming in opposite emotions. For example, you first welcome in a feeling of relaxation and then invite in a feeling of tension. Fighting against emotions that come up leads to conflict and suffering in the mind and body. In order to be mentally well-balanced, you need to be able to welcome and experience *all* emotions. This can be challenging when your emotion is anxiety or fear, but the more you practise accepting and not rejecting these difficult emotions, the more you can let these emotions come and go.

By shifting between opposite emotions you create new coping strategies, your stress dial becomes more flexible and you can build a deeper connection with your body, your emotions and your thoughts. It also enables you to learn to respond to challenging feelings rather than react to them.

Although it may sound too good to be true, the research and evidence continues to grow and it is being used more and more in the treatment of anxiety disorders.[14] As I mentioned above, I have benefitted from using yoga nidra and I can't recommend it enough. I have created a recording for you that focusses on some of the main aspects of this technique. I recommend using it twice a day for the first three weeks in order to lay down new pathways.

Once you start to notice a shift, you can use it once a day if you find it difficult to fit it in twice a day. After you have been using the audio for a while, you can try practising without the recording so that you can use it wherever you are.

Deep Relaxation Practice (Audio 3)

I have made an audio track to guide you through this technique.

Please go to https://www.vivienneemery.com/audio

* Please do not listen to the audio whilst driving or operating heavy machinery.

RAIN technique

The RAIN technique is an extremely effective way of reducing anxiety by learning to control where you put your attention. It is a Buddhist practice that is used to handle a range of emotions, but works particularly well with anxiety. I use it all the time because it stops intense emotions and sensations in their tracks. Instead of identifying with your physical symptoms, it allows you to observe what is going on in your body.

RAIN is an acronym; I have outlined below what the letters stand for.

RAIN

Recognise what you are feeling. It is important to label the emotion. 'Oh, okay, this is my anxiety coming on.' Some people find it helpful to give their anxiety a name. It doesn't seem so threatening when you think, 'Oh, that's just Anxious Alan. What's up Alan?'

Allow the sensations to be there. By accepting and allowing, you will no longer be fighting against these

---

sensations. The more you resist, the more anxious you will feel. They will continue to knock on the door until you open it and listen to what they have to say.

Investigate what the sensations are and where you feel them. Say, 'Okay, I'm listening.' Scan your body. What do you notice? Is your heart rate accelerating? Do you have sensations in the stomach? What does that feel like? Is the sensation in your stomach getting stronger or has it moved to a different area of your body? Do you feel hot or shaky? What is your breath doing? Follow the sensations around the body. Imagine you are a scientist who is curious to know what really goes on when people are anxious. The longer you stand back and observe, the longer the thinking brain will stay online.

Non-identification with your bodily sensations. Avoid getting drawn in by these sensations. Instead of identifying with the fear and going along with it, tell yourself that this is an exercise response at the wrong time and place. Have an open body posture and breathe deeply. Show your body that there is no danger and no need to run or fight right now. Chewing gum can also help because the body switches on your digestion juices and the brain thinks, 'Oh, okay, if we are eating then there can't be any danger.'

Let's imagine you are sitting on a train when you begin to feel your anxiety coming on. Instead of fighting it and getting upset, label it, 'Oh, hi, Anxious Alan' (**Recognise**). Accept that he has come round for a cup of tea; don't shut the door in his face (**Allow**). Observe your sensations, 'Wow, my heart is really going for it, I wonder how much faster it can go' (**Investigate**). Tell yourself that there is no need to be alarmed; your heart would beat this fast if you were running. Show your body there is no danger by relaxing your posture and taking slow breaths (**Non-identification**).

After a couple of minutes, check in with how you are feeling by repeating the process. Where are the sensations now? Are they more or less intense? Welcome all sensations, recognise them, investigate them and continue to show the body there is no danger by having an open posture and using the long breath out technique to stimulate the relaxation response.

Below is a small card version that you can copy and take out with you until you get to know the technique by heart.

RAIN

Recognise and label it. 'Oh, hi, Anxious Alan!'

Allow (don't suppress it). 'Come in, Alan, and have a cup of tea.'

Investigate your sensations. 'Wow, you really are in a state. Tell me more, I'm listening.'

Non-identification. 'Why don't you take a deep breath and leave it to me, Alan? I've got this.'

You may not be able to control when or where your anxiety flares up, but you can control your reaction to it when it does. The RAIN technique gives you a new way to respond. Clients often tell me that this is one of the techniques they use most to prevent their anxiety from escalating so I have made a recording so that you can practise it. Rehearsing this technique whilst you are calm will allow you to build up your ability and confidence in using it so that you can easily remember how to do it when you need it most. Regularly using the RAIN audio and the yoga nidra audio will help you master the skill of observing your bodily sensations rather than getting dragged along with them. The more you can stand outside of these uncomfortable emotions, the more chance you have of keeping your thinking brain online. This is important, as we will discover in Step 4.

The power of your imagination

When we wake up from a nightmare, it is such a relief to realise it wasn't real. There wasn't really a crazed zombie in the house; we imagined it. But if it was just a bad dream, why did we wake up with our heart racing and our nightshirt soaked with sweat? Well, *you* may be aware that is wasn't real but your body didn't know that because it always goes by what the imagination tells it is happening.

The imagination is a powerful resource because the body responds in the same way whether the event is real or imagined. If you were to replay an embarrassing moment from your life right now, you would cringe and feel the same embarrassment even though it happened in the past. The body doesn't know if the event is actually happening right now or not.

It was our ancestors who began to use their imaginations to solve problems by reflecting on what worked in the past and by imagining what could work well in the future. All our best inventions started in someone's imagination. Unfortunately, this amazing tool that nature gave us is often misused when we suffer from anxiety. Instead of using it to imagine a beautiful future, or to reflect on happy moments from our past, we use it to create catastrophic scenarios in our minds of what could happen to us in the future and to constantly replay negative and upsetting events that happened in our past.

The imagination can be a great friend and comfort when we use it wisely, but it is at the heart of your anxiety if you are misusing it. If you start to focus on worrying ideas and images, the body sees them as a real-life threat in the here and now. It tries to help and protect you by activating your fight-or-flight response.

Guided visualisation

A quick and efficient way to switch off your survival response and calm down your nervous system is to change your focus. Instead of imagining things that frighten and upset you, focus your mind on images, events or ideas that make you feel loved, grateful or relaxed. Try the following guided visualisation exercise. Read it through first before you do it.

Change your focus

Close your eyes and bring to mind an image that can cause you discomfort. Maybe it is a past event, or a future event that you are worried about.

Freeze the image in your mind and change the colour so that it is in black and white like an old photograph.

Turn the volume down on the image so that the voices and sounds are muffled.

Now step out of the image so that you are no longer part of it. Shrink the image until it is very small and you can hardly see it.

Now visualise a flash of colour as a new image comes into your mind, an image of someone you love, or a happy memory.

Turn up the volume on the sound and the colours in this scene.

Step into this scene, if you haven't already done so, and feel all the emotions you experienced at that happy time. Notice what emotions you are feeling and where you are feeling them. Go through the scene again and magnify the sensations you can feel in your body.

Visualise success

You may have noticed that the previous exercise asked you to focus on sensations and feelings in your body as you visualised different images. This is because thinking positively is not enough. You may try to tell yourself 'I am calm, I am confident', but when you start to feel anxious it is difficult to believe it. Guided visualisation not only allows you to focus on the positive, it also allows you to feel the physical shift in your body. You need to feel it first to be able to believe it.

When used correctly, guided visualisation is a very powerful technique. It is used by many top sports psychologists and coaches when training elite athletes; for example, a boxer is not only taught to rehearse in their mind how to knock someone out with one punch but to imagine what that would actually feel like.

Long before an actual fight, boxing legend Muhammad Ali always stressed the importance of seeing himself as victorious and what that would feel like. The more an athlete vividly sees himself as the winner, the more their body believes it is possible. Not only does the body start to believe it, but the brain sets up an expectation that the fight or the game will go their way. This is because our brains are designed to seek out and meet expectations once they have been created.

Set up positive expectations in your brain

Have you ever tried to recall a name but couldn't, then three hours later it came to you? The brain has been searching for the answer ever since you asked the question. You set up an expectation and then carried on with your day but your brain didn't stop looking for it. The brain is designed to meet the expectations that you give it.

Imagine you are feeling nervous about giving a speech at a wedding. Every time you think about this future event, you see yourself going red and stumbling over your words.

Every time you do this, you are setting up an expectation in your brain for this to happen. Instead, close your eyes and see the speech going well. See yourself standing there in front of every one with a calm and collected posture. See yourself finishing the speech to a round of applause. Then, when the day comes to give the speech and you stand up in front of everyone, the brain says, 'Hey, I know this scenario and how it should go.'

This is why athletes visualise success over and over again. They see themselves finishing first, they see themselves holding the medal. Top athletes don't train for years then hope and pray they will feel good and in the zone on the day. They programme their minds to go automatically into a winning mindset when they need it. They *expect* to win and they do.

Take back control by setting up the right expectation in the brain

I have created a guided visualisation audio that will help you take back control when you start to feel extremely anxious. It uses the RAIN technique mentioned above, and with regular practice it will help you to set up a new way to respond to your anxiety. The audio will guide you through using this technique, which will allow you to see and feel yourself taking back control. It will set up a new expectation in your brain about how to respond when you are feeling anxious.

It is important to use this audio when you are calm, not when you are in the middle of an anxiety attack. You are creating new pathways in the brain so that your brain remembers the training from the audio when your anxiety is in full swing and uses the RAIN technique automatically and successfully. The more you practise this technique, the more confident you will feel putting it into action when you need it.

Guided visualisation practice (Audio 4)

I have made an audio track to guide you through this technique.

Please go to https://www.vivienneemery.com/audio

* Please do not listen to the audio whilst driving or operating heavy machinery.

Some clients tell me that they can't visualise. Although it is true that some people are more creative than others in what they can see and visualise, everyone has an imagination. If I asked you to imagine a red car with green wheels, you would be able to bring this image to mind. Try not to worry that there must be a right or wrong way to do these techniques; the way in which you create images in your mind will be just right for you.

Repetition is key

Visualisation is only the first step; the second step is repetition. The only way to master a skill is through repetition. The people that stay stuck are the ones who say, 'Oh yes, I've tried this type of exercise *once* before but it wasn't really for me.'

The brain is a mass of millions of neural pathways. Whenever we do something new, we create a new pathway. With repetition, we make a groove so that we can access this behaviour again and again and it becomes automatic. Neurons that fire together, wire together. The brain can form connections to anything, even when it is not logical. I have had a bar of dark chocolate with a cup of tea for so many years now that when I have the tea on its own, my brain goes, 'Seriously? Where's the dark chocolate?'

The human brain is amazing and *your* brain is no different, so try to listen to the audio at least once a day for three weeks in order to create new brain pathways. The more you practise, the more automatic this way of responding will become. Only by doing something over and over again will you create a new habit.

Calm the mind and body by slowing down your brain waves

One of the reasons why these relaxation techniques are effective is because they slow down the frequency of your brain waves. Brain waves are caused by electrical activity in the brain. When we are asleep, we are in a very slow brain wave state called delta. As we wake up in the morning, we move up from delta (a deep restorative sleep state) to theta state (a relaxed state that has a healing effect on the body), then to alpha (a creative, imaginative, dream-like state). Finally we move into beta (a relaxed, awake state).

We move back down through these brain-wave frequencies when we go to sleep at night.

We naturally move in and out of these frequencies during the day. For example, when we daydream, we start to move down to alpha and theta wave frequencies. When we are stressed, anxious and too alert, we are at the higher end of beta. This is not a healthy place to be long term. When you are stuck in high beta, your thinking ability reduces and you can experience intrusive and racing thoughts.

If you are anxious and stressed for most of the day, use the audios and techniques to calm your nervous system and to slow down your brain waves so that you move out of high beta into alpha and theta frequencies.

The theta brain wave (also known as the Rapid Eye Movement or REM state)

In his book *The Biology of Belief*, Bruce Lipton explains that because the theta brain wave state is our natural learning state, it is a useful frequency to access in therapy.[16] The brain is particularly receptive during theta, and we naturally enter this state when we learn something that we didn't know before.

Brain scans have shown that children function on the theta wave frequency until the age of seven. Being in this state allows children to download an extremely high volume of information so as to thrive in their own environment.

Children need to download information quickly because, unlike guinea pigs, human babies are not born ready to go out and function in the world. Although being in theta state is useful, it also means children end up downloading negative beliefs and values from their parents, siblings, teachers and peers without questioning them. We download these beliefs straight into the subconscious mind, where they stay unchallenged. If you grow up constantly being told you are stupid, worthless and unlovable, it can be very hard to shift these beliefs as an adult. We may also grow up with biased beliefs about how the world works, for example that people are violent, people can't be trusted, the world is a dangerous place, love is painful.

As an adult, trying to shift these downloaded beliefs using the conscious mind can prove challenging. This is why using positive affirmations on their own is often ineffective. Your conscious mind only has 5% control over what you say and do, whereas the unconscious mind has 95% control. The quickest way to update these beliefs is to talk directly with the unconscious mind. You can do this by accessing the theta wave state (the natural learning state in your unconscious mind). Different techniques are used to enter this natural learning state during therapy including guided relaxation, guided meditation, guided visualisation and hypnosis.

How do guided visualisation and guided relaxation relate to hypnosis?

Meditation, visualisation, hypnosis and other mind-body approaches use relaxation techniques such as breathing, body sensing and imagery to stimulate the relaxation response and to calm the brain waves. These practices turn your attention inwards and narrow your focus, which allows you to access alpha and then theta brain waves.

The difference between these practices is what you do when you are in this theta state. In meditation, you still the mind and observe your thoughts and sensations so it is usually a passive practice. During guided visualisation you take a more active role, rehearse new behaviours and consider ways to solve problems. In hypnosis, suggestions are made to the client in order to update unwanted beliefs and behaviours.

Binaural beat therapy

Binaural beat therapy uses headphones to deliver a different auditory signal to each ear; the brain then blends the two sounds into a single tone. The beats are designed to change your brain waves and help you move out of high beta and into alpha and theta.

It is becoming popular to record guided relaxation meditations with binaural beats in the background. It is claimed that this can help maintain good mental health and reduce anxiety and stress. You can find free binaural beat audios on the internet. All you need to do is put on some headphones, sit in a relaxed position and listen to the beats. It is a good idea to check the frequency of the binaural beats in the recording before using it because sometimes the tracks can turn out to be higher or lower than indicated.

Although most people can use binaural beats with no harmful consequences, I chose not to use them in any of the audios because there are certain groups of people that should avoid them. If you suffer from epilepsy or cardiac issues, you need to use them with caution. It is best to talk to your doctor beforehand if you are not sure.

Another reason why they have not been used in my audios is because individuals may have different reactions when listening to binaural beats. Despite many people finding the beats very useful, there are others who find them irritating, confusing and ineffective.

Practise mindfulness during the day

Mindfulness doesn't require training; it is nothing fancy and it can be practised anytime, anywhere. It is simply allowing yourself to observe and experience emotions in the present moment without judgement. You could notice the feel of the clothes on your skin, or a breeze on your face. When you eat something, you could focus on the textures of the food. When you take a shower, you could focus on the sensation of the water on your skin. When you are stuck in traffic you could notice how angry you feel and where you feel this anger most – in your chest, in your stomach, in your head. There are thousands of ways you can observe your experience in the present moment. The more you observe and pay attention to what you are doing and feeling, the more natural it becomes.

What are the benefits?

Being mindful builds your resilience to stress and anxiety because you shift from *identifying* with what you feel to *observing* what you feel. It is not about fixing what you are feeling but rather allowing it to be there and observing it. This is what lies behind the RAIN technique.

There are a number of benefits reported by people who practise mindfulness regularly.

1. It settles your mind.

Mindfulness promotes a more balanced outlook on life. You have more control over where you place your attention, and it reduces how much you bounce around from one thought to the next. It allows you to take control by focussing on positive images rather than on negative ones. This, in turn, will change your state.

2. It increases your self-awareness.

Mindfulness trains you to become aware of what is going on inside your body and mind. It shows you how you respond to external events. For example, how angry do you feel when you get stuck in traffic? How do you know you are angry? What sensations do you feel and where do you feel them? Do you react and say something aggressive? The more aware you become, and the more in tune you are with your inner disturbances, the more you will be able to intervene and prevent these strong emotions from escalating. Instead of identifying with your anger, you can smile at yourself for blowing this situation out of proportion. You can remind yourself that feeling this way isn't helping; what's worse, it is adding to your stress levels. When you intervene like this, you prevent strong emotions from escalating.

3. It teaches you to be less reactive.

By observing and being more aware of thoughts and feelings and how they make you feel, you become more detached; you can take control and respond rather than react. You stop seeing life events as catastrophic.

Over time, this also increases your compassion for others. Most of us would do anything for the people that we love but we constantly hurt them by losing control over how we feel and how we react.

With continued use of mindfulness, you will find you begin to move away from impulsive negative reactions and choose your battles wisely. This will have a positive knock-on effect on your personal relationships, your health and your ability to bounce back from stress.

Mindfulness exercise

Choose an activity from your morning routine to pay mindful attention to – this could be cleaning your teeth, taking a shower, eating your breakfast, etc. These are times the mind can wander the most. Take control of your attention and notice the feel of the water on your skin or the sensation of the brush on your teeth. Try this for a week, then add in a second task from your day. You can do as many tasks as you want to, but try to commit to being mindful to at least one task a day.

As well as focussing on a specific task, also start to become mindful of your own reactions and thoughts about the world around you. Notice what you are thinking and feeling when you are stuck in a queue, or when someone is rude to you. Don't identify with your thoughts and feelings, just observe them.

Use the table below to keep a record of your thoughts and feelings when you focus on a specific task and for events that are happening around you. I have provided a couple of examples to help you get started.

What was the task/activity or challenging situation?	What did you notice and feel during this activity/situation? What were some of your thoughts?	Before you finish this activity, write in the box below what you are feeling in your body right now
Taking a shower		
Being stuck in traffic		
?		
?		
?		

Step 3 takeaways

1. Guided relaxation not only shrinks your fight-or-flight centre but also calms your nervous system.

2. Engage your thinking brain by observing your sensations instead of identifying with them. Use the RAIN technique to help you do this.

3. Your imagination is a powerful tool. We feel what we focus on. If you run worrying images through your mind, you will activate your fight-or-flight response. Change your focus to change the way you feel.

4. Use guided visualisation to rehearse taking back control during an anxiety attack. Guided visualisation is used by top athletes because it is a powerful way to set up a winning mindset.

5. Repetition is the only way to master a skill. Listen regularly to the audios and practise the techniques often to form new pathways in your brain. Over time, these healthier ways of responding to stress and anxiety will become automatic.

6. It is just as important to calm your brain waves as it is to relax the body.

7. Theta (or REM) state is your natural learning state. Use relaxation techniques to access this brain wave because when we are in this frequency we can talk directly to the unconscious mind and update beliefs and behaviours.

8. Binaural beat therapy is used to relax your brain. Although it is considered safe when used for therapeutic reasons, check with your doctor first.

9. Mindfulness is another way to teach yourself to observe your anxiety rather than identify with it. Start to observe how you react and feel in different situations and whilst doing different tasks.

STEP 4

Why is it so difficult to challenge my thoughts?

Where did my intelligence go?

Have you ever been tongue tied? I remember my first school trip to France when I was a teenager. I had spent a couple of years studying French and felt ready to practise it in a local shop. I found a small bakery and went inside. As soon as the shop assistant asked me what I wanted, I started to panic. My mind went completely blank and I couldn't even think of one French word. I went bright red, turned around and walked out. Once I was back on the street, all the sentences I wanted to say came flooding into my brain, 'A bit late, now,' I thought.

In Step 1, we looked at how powerful the emotional brain can be when we are fearful. It can reduce your thinking ability when you are anxious, and even switch it off completely when you are really afraid, such as in a life-or-death emergency.

Let's have a closer look at what is going on so that you can take back control and keep it engaged for longer.

The reptile brain, the emotional brain and the thinking brain

As the brain is incredibly complex, American neuroscientist Paul Maclean came up with a simple way of looking at it. He divided the brain into three layers. At the bottom is our oldest layer, the ancient part that evolved in reptiles; we will call this layer the 'reptile brain' because it has the same wiring as a lizard's brain. It regulates all your involuntary processes, such as body temperature, heartbeat, breath, etc. On top of that is layer two, the limbic system. This layer is responsible for all your emotions, so let's call it your 'emotional brain'. The third layer at the top is the cortex, the most highly developed part of the human brain; let's call this our 'thinking brain'.

Bottom-up processing

So far, we have seen that the direction of control when we are fearful is bottom up. The reptile brain notices a difference in your breathing and heart rate and sends a message to the emotional brain that there must be danger present. The emotional brain activates the fight-or-flight response and turns the thinking brain down or off. It is therefore true that our minds go completely blank when we feel nervous or anxious.

Exam stress can make someone sit for a whole hour staring at a question, not able to write anything because their mind has gone blank. Their emotions are so high that the thinking brain has gone offline. The emotional brain stays on and is in charge, but it has limited thinking ability because when we are in danger the choice is simplistic: run away, or stay and fight. This rigid, limited way of thinking is known as 'all-or-nothing' thinking.

Anxiety and all-or-nothing thinking

When we are anxious, we may not be in a life-or-death situation but we *are* fearful. The body senses fear and wants to protect us, so it turns up the emotional brain's functioning and turns down the thinking brain's functioning. As a result, your thoughts, beliefs, decisions and language become very rigid: 'I'm always anxious'; 'I am a useless person'; 'Life is awful'. Your thoughts are very black and white because your emotional brain is in charge of your thinking.

It can be very difficult to challenge these all-or-nothing thoughts whilst you are still anxious. This is why many people feel frustrated when they are told to do just that.

Showing people how to control their thoughts before showing them how to control and calm down their bodies is like teaching someone to dive before they know how to swim. The first three steps in this book were about teaching you how to swim and the different strokes you can use. Once you feel comfortable in the water, you can then master the dive. You won't be able to dive effectively if you are still fearful of the water.

Top-down processing

Once the thinking brain is back online, cognitive therapy techniques are very effective. We have seen that the command of control can go bottom up when the emotional brain takes over, but it is also possible to go top down when the thinking brain is online. When we are calm, we can use our thoughts to send messages to the body that everything is okay. We can think of happy memories or list things we are grateful for. As soon as we change our focus, we change how we feel. Being able to master your thoughts and what you focus on is a very powerful tool, and it is why cognitive therapy (when used with relaxation therapy) can be highly effective.

The feeling-thought-feeling loop

We can see that there is a loop. Your feelings affect your thoughts, and your thoughts affect your feelings. The more we work on calming the nervous system, the more we can work on changing our thoughts; the more control we have over our thoughts, the more we can shift our focus away from fear and panic, and send out relaxing thoughts and messages to the body, which continue to calm it down. For example, you notice you are feeling on edge and so you start your breathing exercises. As the body calms down, you focus on a happy memory. The body remembers this memory and a wave of happiness spreads throughout the body, which relaxes the nervous system even more.

Unfortunately, what often happens in anxiety is that we use this loop in a destructive way and end up feeling more anxious. For example, you start to feel on edge and the sensations make you fearful. Your thinking brain is turned down low and your emotional brain takes over and tells you that something must be wrong. You start to create worrying images in your head. These thoughts and images send alarm messages to the body, which fuel the anxiety response and the loop continues.

Instead of identifying with the bodily sensations and being alarmed by them, be inquisitive and use the RAIN technique from Step 3. This will allow you to stay in control, 'talk' to your anxiety and send messages that everything is okay. It will prevent the sensations from escalating.

Train your brain to focus on the positive

One of the reasons we all have negative thoughts is because we are working with a two-million-year-old brain that has evolved to look for problems and danger. It is automatic for us to focus on the negative because in the past it saved our lives. If our ancestors saw a snake-like stick, they would jump without thinking; the brain is programmed to assume the worse. Once you have moved out of harm's way and noticed that it was only a stick, the brain says, 'Oh well, better safe than sorry.' If you fuel this way of thinking by also focussing on the negative and all the terrible things that have happened to you (and could possibly happen to you in the future) you will get stuck in a negative pattern of only looking for what is wrong. These thoughts will help to drive your anxiety.

We need to recondition the brain to also focus on the positive. You can't stop a negative thought coming up but you can decide what to do with it. You have a choice; you can get caught up in this thought and begin to stack up negative ideas and images in your mind, or you can change your focus and deliberately bring to mind an image of someone or something you love.

An effective way to shift your attention is to focus on something in your life that you appreciate. It may sound corny but it really is a useful practice. Some people like to start and end their day with three things they are grateful for; others use a gratitude journal. The more you train your brain to focus on the positive aspects in your life, the more of a habit it becomes.

In Step 3, we spoke about how powerful the imagination is. Whether a scene is imagined or real makes no difference to your body; it will feel what you imagine. This is why your mood will match what you are focussed on. If you are focussed on all the negative things in your life, guess what your mood will be like.

The law of attraction was a concept first written about in 1906 by William Walker Atkinson. He stated that what you focus on is what you get.[17] If you focus on being successful, the chances are you will be. If you focus on the fear of having an anxiety attack and how awful the sensations will be, the brain will fixate on this and the more anxious you will feel.

Is it really that simple to change how you feel? If your thinking brain is online, then yes, it is. You will feel what you think about vividly. The exercise in Step 3 asked you to close your eyes and think about a happy memory or someone you love. When you do this, you will release a wave of happy chemicals and feel them everywhere. The challenge is to stay in this relaxed and positive state. To do this, you need to make it a habit by learning to stack the positive experiences, images and memories on top of each other.

Where is your focus at the moment? Are you focussed on all the things you can't control and can't change and what you don't want in life, or are you focussed on what you can change, what you can control and what you do want in life?

It is not about being an optimist

An optimist fell from a tenth-storey window. At each window he passed on his way down, he called out cheerfully to the people inside, 'Doing all right so far!'

I am not telling you that everything will be fine if you use positive thinking. Nor am I telling you to be an optimist; if it is raining outside, then it is raining. It's important to acknowledge when things are not going well; the key is not to get stuck there and not to see things as worse than they really are. Learn to change how you are feeling by changing what you focus on. If it is raining and you can't do what you had planned, do you focus on that and feel down or do you focus on how fun it would be to stay in and catch up on that new TV series, or make that cake you've been wanting to try out?

Everyone experiences negative emotions and thoughts no matter how positive they are. The people who stay resilient are the ones who don't get stuck in a negativity loop. They change their focus and are able to have just as many, if not more, positive emotions and thoughts as negative ones. With practice and repetition, it is more than possible to recondition the brain to look for the positives as well as the negatives.

Stop fighting against unwanted thoughts

Your brain produces over 65,000 thoughts a day; that's an average of 2,700 thoughts an hour. Every thought you have influences your life. Every thought you have will have a direct effect on the way you feel. One thought enables you to believe that you are capable of great things, whilst another makes you feel worthless, unlovable and not likely to amount to anything.

Trying to stop yourself from thinking certain thoughts never works. If I said to you, 'Don't think about a tortoise wearing glasses and reading a book,' what happens? You can't help but see an image of a rather intelligent-looking tortoise. Even if you can avoid it for a few seconds you are aware that the thought is there, waiting for you to bump into it.

Why can't you stop unwanted thoughts on command?

For the brain *not* to think about something, it needs to know what it isn't allowed to think about, otherwise how can it avoid it? It therefore keeps the intelligent-looking tortoise nearby in your thoughts so that you know that when you see it, you must avoid it. That may seem annoying but it is yet another example of how helpful your mind and body are trying to be for you.

What's the answer then?

Let your brain know that your unwanted anxious thoughts are not important to you. The only way to do this is to stop fighting and blocking them. Allow them in, then let them go. I mentioned that we don't have any control over which unwanted thoughts come up – but we do have control over what we decide to do with them.

Unwanted thoughts will continue to surface if you:

1. Try to block them.

The more you resist and try to avoid them, the more they will lurk in the background like that image of the tortoise. Remember, the brain is trying to be helpful. The brain says, 'Okay, you don't want to think about that. Well, I'd better just leave it here in the corner so that you won't forget what it is you don't want to think about!'

2. Keep spinning unwanted thoughts around in your head.

The more time you spend on a thought, the more important the brain believes it to be. Consequently, it will keep throwing it up. It will say, 'Ooh, you haven't thought about this in the last ten minutes. I know how you normally spend a lot of time thinking about it, so here it is again. The last time I brought it up, you spent a whole thirty-five minutes thinking about it, so it must be important.'

You can't stop an unwanted thought but the less time you spend with this thought, the less often the brain will throw it into your consciousness. It will take time and practice, but you can follow certain steps to show the brain that this thought is not important to you and it doesn't need to keep bringing it up.

First, identify the thought when it comes and label it. 'Oh, that's my "I wish I hadn't said that to my boss" thought.' Once you have done this, you can bring in a different thought that you like to think about to replace it: an image of someone you love, a happy memory, a scene from a movie you like, a song. It doesn't matter what it is, it's just important to get into the habit of replacing the unwanted thought with a wanted one. When you do this, you only spend a few seconds on the unwanted thought. It comes up and then goes away when you replace it with something positive and the brain no longer sees it as important to you.

These steps allow you to accept the thought, observe it and let it go so that it doesn't hang around for too long. This is what normally happens to everyday random thoughts that come and go and don't trouble you. Your unwanted thoughts are bothering you because you are either resisting them or hanging on to them for too long.

Have you ever gone through a bad break up where you spent weeks, if not months, thinking about that person all day, every day? After some time, you notice that a whole day has passed by and you haven't thought about them.

Then a whole week, a whole year, until you rarely think about them. In fact, the only time you do think of them is when you occasionally wonder to yourself if they have now gained lots of weight and developed halitosis.

The number of thoughts you had about this ex-partner started to reduce because you didn't spend as much time dwelling on each thought that came up, and because other thoughts started to replace them. Thoughts about a new partner in your life, or about new dreams and plans. Over time, your brain stopped bringing up your ex-partner because it no longer saw them as important. The brain took its cue from you; it no longer saw them as important because you spent less time mulling over the thoughts when they came up.

Let's recap that point because it is very important.

Although we don't initially control which unwanted thoughts arise, we can learn to control how often they arise and how long they stay around. We can do this by:

1. No longer dwelling on them when they come up

2. Replacing them with other thoughts.

Take a moment to write down a thought that you have on a regular basis that causes you stress and anxiety. How do you feel when it comes up? How do you usually respond? How long do you usually stay with this thought? What keeps it there? Do you stack up other anxious thoughts to go with it?

Now, come up with a thought, image, memory or scene from a movie that you could use to replace this unwanted thought. Practise doing this a couple of times and then use the steps below to help you when these unwanted thoughts arise during the day.

Dealing with anxious thoughts

1. Allow the unwanted thought to come in. Don't resist it.

2. Label the thought 'This is my ... thought'.

3. Avoid getting angry or frustrated. Change your focus instead. Have a positive thought ready to replace it – it could be a positive image of someone you love, a happy memory, a scene from a movie you like or you could bring a song into your head. Prepare this image or thought in advance and always use this one so that it becomes a habit. Choose something that makes you smile and feel good inside.

4. If the unwanted thought comes straight back again, that's okay. Breathe and repeat the steps. At first it will continue to come up, and

---

> sometimes you will get caught up in it without realising. That's okay. If you say, 'Oh no, I just got caught up with it again,' that's a good sign. The more you are consciously aware of what is going on, the more progress you will make.

Don't expect to have instant results, especially if this unwanted thought has been hanging around for a while. It will keep trying to reel you in. The brain isn't being cruel, it just can't understand why you no longer want to think about it. It says, 'No, look at it again. You love thinking about this. Don't be so hasty.' You have to recondition the brain so that, over time, it understands that this thought is no longer important. It may take time and practise but it is worth it, especially if your anxious thoughts have been bothering you for a while.

If you continue to focus on positive images and emotions, the brain will start to bring more of these up on a regular basis. It will start to say, 'Look, at this happy memory I've found. You seem to want to look at happy memories – how about this one?' It is a great memory, and you spend fifteen minutes thinking about it and going over it in your mind. The brain thinks, 'Oh, you really think this kind of thing is important so I'll find another one just like it.'

We get so frustrated with our anxious thoughts but the brain doesn't have a mind of its own – it is your mind! The sooner you change where you put your focus, the sooner your brain will follow suit. Your thoughts won't change until you make a conscious effort to change what you focus on.

Jack had spent most of his life trying to block his unwanted thoughts. When he started to use this technique, it was difficult at first to allow in replacement images without putting up some resistance but over time he got better at it. When I asked him what image he used to replace his unwanted thoughts, he told me it was always the same image of himself scoring the winning penalty goal for his local football team. He said that he could replay that scene over and over all day.

It is important to choose an image or thought that is compelling like Jack's because the more interesting it is, the easier it will be to move away from the disturbing thought.

Thought awareness practice (Audio 5)

I have made an audio track to guide you through this technique.

Please go to https://www.vivienneemery.com/audio

* Please do not listen to the audio whilst driving or operating heavy machinery.

Have a worry time

If you find you are worrying the whole day about a situation, you can set aside a worry time, for example, in the morning between 10am and 10.20am. When a worrying thought comes up, write it down and say, 'I won't think about this now, I will think about it during my worry time.' Repeat this process every time a new or old worry comes up.

This is particularly useful if anxious thoughts are keeping you awake. Turn on the light, write them down and tell yourself, 'I will think about this during my worry time.' When your worry time comes, set your alarm for 20 minutes and worry about all the points on your list. When the alarm goes off, stop. If you come up with any solutions to your problems during that time, that's great; if not, tell yourself, 'I can't do anything about it now, I will think about it again tomorrow during my worry time.'

People often find that when they sit down deliberately to worry the brain soon gets bored with this activity and they start to worry less.

If you can do something about your worries, write down what you will do and when. If there is nothing you can do, tell yourself, 'I can't do anything about this problem. I have no control over it but I do have control over where I put my focus.' The more certain you are that you can change your focus, the more confident and less fearful you will be. Self-confidence comes from being certain of yourself and how you will manage, despite what is going on around you.

Remind yourself of how resourceful you are

Sometimes we can get stuck in negative thought loops where we doubt our abilities and our strengths: 'I am not a confident person'; 'I am a nervous person'; 'I am not very brave'. It is therefore important to remind yourself often of what you have achieved in the past and the resources that you had (and still have) that allowed you to succeed and overcome difficulties.

A friend of mine had a difficult homelife when she was growing up. From the age of ten, she had taken on the parent role to both her brother and her mother because her mother was an alcoholic. She managed to get herself through school and in her last year she applied to study at a local college. She needed a character reference and asked one of the teachers that she was close to if he could write one for her. When she read the reference, she couldn't believe what he had written. The teacher had described her in such a positive and glowing light that at first she thought he'd written it for someone else. The reference spoke of her courage and determination, and how she always went out of her way to help others. Having received little praise from anyone at home, it was the first time she had seen herself in this way.

For twenty years she has kept a copy of that reference in a drawer at home. Every now and then, when she is feeling less confident, useless or doubts herself, she takes it out and reads it to remind herself of all she has been through, how she has overcome so much, and that she does have strengths and resources. Even if it has been a while since she has felt resilient or capable, she knows that she has felt these emotions in the past and, if she has felt them in the past, there is no reason why she can't feel them again.

I have many clients who tell me how fearful they are and that they wish they were brave like other people they know. I remind them of all the things they continue to do despite their anxiety.

'Do you go to the shops even though you are fearful?'

'Yes,' they say.

'Do you go into work, despite all the anxiety you feel the night before and in the morning?'

'Yes,' they say.

Isn't that the very definition of bravery? If you don't have fear, there is no need for courage. Courage is being extremely fearful of doing something, but doing it anyway.

So, take a moment now to write down your strengths. Maybe life is difficult and you are feeling highly anxious, but take a moment to think back to times in the past when you overcame your fears. If you find it difficult, see yourself though the eyes of someone who loves you. What would they say about you? Think about how you have coped so far with your anxiety. If you are still here, then you have coped. How have you managed to get through the days? How have you managed to keep going despite everything? Who do you continue to show up for – your children, your partner? This takes guts and strength of character. Tap into your own unique resourcefulness.

What have been your successes in life? Write them down and keep them nearby so that when you have doubts you can remind yourself who you are and who you have been. Ask questions, such as, 'What is going well in my life or has gone well in the past?' Build on your past achievements to enhance your confidence and self-esteem.

Use the chart on the next page to help you make a record of your resources.

Your qualities and strengths	Achievements and successes	Difficulties in the past that you have overcome
I am…	I have…	When facing this (state your challenging life event), I got through it by…
I am…	I have…	When facing this (state your challenging life event), I got through it by…
I am…	I have…	When facing this (state your challenging life event), I got through it by…
I am…	I have…	When facing this (state your challenging life event), I got through it by…

Step 4 takeaways

1. The emotional brain turns the thinking brain down or off when we are anxious.

2. When the emotional brain is in charge, we resort to 'all or nothing' thinking patterns.

3. Calming the nervous system switches the thinking brain back on, which means we can use top-down processing, i.e. we can now use our thoughts to change the way we feel.

4. When we focus on positive thoughts we change our focus, which then changes the way we feel. This is a healthy loop cycle to get into. The more positive we feel, the calmer our nervous systems will be, which means our thinking brain stays on for longer.

5. Manage unwanted thoughts by accepting them rather than rejecting them. Once they are invited in, you can replace them with a more positive thought.

6. Schedule in a 'worry time' each day to reduce the amount of stress and anxiety that can build up from having worrisome thoughts all day.

7. Remind yourself often of your resources, strengths and past achievements.

STEP 5

How do I create lasting change?

Be stress ready

To really benefit from making any change in your life, it has to be lasting and consistent. Regularly taking time for yourself and allowing your mind and body to rest and restore creates the foundation for your resilience to stress. Working with a full cup rather than an empty one will enable you to bounce back from physical and mental stress.

As well as using the audios and the exercises to calm the nervous system and master our thought patterns, we also need to consider how other factors, such as lack of sleep, lack of exercise and a poor diet, could begin to push our stress and anxiety levels back up again without us realising it.

Anxiety and sleep

I don't need to tell you that sleep is important. How much sleep we get at night is a huge factor in how we feel mentally and physically. For many years and in many cultures, sleep deprivation has been used as one of the most effective forms of torture. It might not be as violent as cutting off someone's finger, but it does far more damage because it slowly attacks all the biological functions in the mind and body. When taken to the extreme, sleep deprivation will result in death.

We know this, yet how many of us at night stifle a yawn and decide to watch one more film or play one more computer game? We torture our bodies by denying ourselves the maximum hours possible to rest and restore. It may seem dramatic but the more you force yourself to function in the day with a cup half full, the more stress you put on the body. One of the best ways to strengthen your physical resilience to stress is through sleep.

It is not necessarily the amount you sleep but the *quality* of sleep you get that is important. Two extremely important stages we go through whilst asleep are slow-wave sleep, and dream sleep or REM (Rapid Eye Movement) sleep.

You need slow-wave sleep to restore the body and renew your energy; you need dream sleep or REM sleep to discharge unexpressed emotional arousals from the day.[18] If you wake up feeling exhausted, you could be spending too much time in REM sleep. If you are prone to feeling unwell and suffering from aches and pains, it is a possible sign that you are not getting enough slow-wave sleep.

The importance of slow-wave sleep

Slow-wave sleep repairs bodily tissues and sweeps out brain debris. It helps to restore the body from the wear and tear of the day. The brain cells are recharged and the immune system is boosted. If you are not in slow-wave sleep for a sufficient amount of time, your body cannot remove the waste from your tired brain cells. Cognitive decline, dementia and other brain conditions can develop if the waste isn't taken away properly.

When the immune system isn't restored and boosted during sleep, you become more vulnerable to sickness and life-threatening illnesses. You also become more susceptible to fibromyalgia because while you sleep your body also works on restoring energy and nutrients to worn-out muscles and tissues.

The importance of dream sleep (REM sleep)

Even if we don't remember our dreams, we all go through REM cycles every night when we sleep; all mammals do. We have to do this in order to release the arousals from the day. Dream sleep is not restful sleep; electroencephalogram (EEG) recordings show brain-wave activity during REM sleep is the same as when we are awake. If we have a frightening dream, the body releases cortisol and speeds up the heart as if you were being frightened in real life. After many years of research, Joe Griffin showed that the role of dreaming is to deactivate the unexpressed emotional arousals from the day.[18] Dream sleep destresses our system so that we can start afresh the next day.

It is vital that we enter REM (or dream) sleep to process arousals from the day. However, on average we should only spend around two hours during the night going in and out of REM sleep; any more than this and there is not enough time left to spend in slow-wave sleep. If you are stressed and anxious and suffer from more than your fair share of arousals during the day, real or imagined, your body and mind need to spend longer in REM sleep to destress your system.

This is problematic for two reasons.

1. REM sleep is not restful sleep; your body plays out scenarios in your dreams to release unexpressed arousals from the day and your body reacts as if they are real.

2. If you spend too long dreaming, you can wake up feeling exhausted. You feel more tired than when you went to bed.

People who suffer from anxiety and depression often find themselves waking up in the early hours of the morning unable to get to sleep again. They have a lot of unexpressed anxious thoughts and emotions during the day and therefore need to spend a long time in REM sleep to discharge the arousals. The body and brain become exhausted; they can't continue to process all your arousals and decide that it is better to wake you up than continue to stay in REM sleep.[18]

You can read more about Joe Griffin's ideas on dream sleep and depression in the e-book titled *Stop telling me to cheer up.* You can download it for free at www.vivienneemery.com.

How can I reduce my REM sleep and increase my slow-wave sleep?

If you find yourself waking up exhausted in the morning after sleeping for seven hours or so, you have probably had too much REM sleep. This could be a sign that you need to rest and restore more during the day.

I know I am beginning to sound like a broken record but the answer is to take the time to de-stress the body throughout day. If you work on releasing some of your anxiety and stress during the day, there is less to deal with at night. We have already looked at how to do this in previous steps. You can take a few minutes several times a day to close your eyes and stimulate your relaxation response using the breathing techniques, and you can find twenty-five minutes in your day (twice a day, if you can) to listen to a guided relaxation to deeply relax the body.

As well as having moments of rest and recovery in your day, you also need to reduce the number of worrying thoughts that you get caught up in. Start using the techniques in Step 4 to cut down on the time you spend mulling over anxious thoughts.

Sometimes at night when we are lying in bed, our minds can really get going and start bringing up one worry after another. This activity will elevate the brain waves into a high beta frequency and it will be nearly impossible to sleep. This is a reason why anxiety can cause insomnia.

People often put on the TV or read a book when they can't get to sleep. Yes, that can be useful for some, but for many it will continue to keep their brainwaves active. It is better to close your eyes and listen to the radio or a relaxation audio. You need to shut out as much stimulation as possible because 80% of information comes in from the eyes. The quickest way to reduce the frequency of your brain waves is to shut out the external world. Looking at your phone is the worst thing you can do before going to bed, especially if you read an email or message that upsets you. This is another arousal you have added to the long list of other ones that need to be processed during dream sleep.

Follow your body's natural rhythms

The body and the mind follow a circadian rhythm. This is a natural, internal process that regulates the sleep-wake cycle and is repeated every 24 hours. At night time, when we lie in bed and close our eyes, we should fall asleep within 10 to 20 minutes. If you are not asleep after 45 minutes this could be for a number of reasons.

1. You are getting too much sleep during the day, or you are sleeping in too late in the morning.

2. You have come to bed too early.

3. You are stressed and anxious and are unable to calm down your body and mind.

As well as resting and relaxing the mind and body during the day, you can also try the audio below to help you drift off to sleep. You will notice that some of the steps are similar to the practice of yoga nidra and other guided relaxation techniques. That's because all these techniques mimic the natural process of slowing down the mind and body to enable it to rest and sleep.

The aim of the audio is to follow what your body does naturally when it begins the process of falling asleep. It is not helpful to force yourself to sleep when your thoughts are racing and the body is releasing adrenalin. You need to relax the body and calm the mind instead.

If you are still awake after listening to the audio, that's okay. It may take some time to retrain your natural process of falling asleep, so simply get up and press play again.

If you have had insomnia for a long time, you may need to practise for a number of weeks before the brain starts to create a new pattern for you. Please avoid trying it once and giving up because it didn't work for you. It takes time, effort and repetition to create new pathways in the brain.

Even when you don't sleep whilst listening to the audio, you will be relaxing your body; this is better than lying there getting stressed and frustrated and willing yourself to sleep. Listening to a relaxation audio at night can be more restful than a night of restless sleep. The more you practise activating your natural process of falling asleep, the easier it will become and the better quality of sleep you will have.

Audio for sleep (Bonus audio)

I have made an audio track to guide you through this technique. Please go to www.vivienneemery.com

* Please do not listen to the audio whilst driving or operating heavy machinery.

Don't marinate in your stress hormones!

If this technique is taking a while to work and two hours later you are still lying in bed wide awake with your thoughts racing, you MUST get up! You may be thinking, 'I don't want to get up. It's cold, and I'm sure if I just try for a few minutes more, I will fall asleep.' However, you will never slow the brain waves down by just lying there with your thoughts racing. Your body and mind are winding each other up: the more cortisol that is released, the more anxious you feel; the more anxious you feel, the longer you will stay awake; the longer you stay awake the more anxious you get about not being asleep by now.

Get up! You are doing more harm than good lying there marinating in your stress hormones. It is better to get up than lie there feeling anxious.

When you get up, do something boring. Don't watch TV or have a snack; it is not a good idea to reward the brain for being awake, otherwise you will create an unhelpful pattern. Instead, get up and read a boring news article or rearrange your kitchen cupboards. Do something you usually don't enjoy. Eventually the brain will think, 'Do you know what, I'd rather be asleep.' It won't think this if you are watching your favourite film whilst eating ice cream! Break the habit of insomnia by punishing the brain. Do something mind-numbingly boring so that it no longer *wants* to be awake.

As the brain becomes bored, you will start yawning. When you do, get back into bed. If you are still awake 30 minutes later, get up again. You need to retrain your brain. It may take many attempts and many nights, but eventually it will learn that night time is for sleeping. The brain won't switch off whilst you are anxious; it stays awake to protect you because it thinks you are in danger. Show your brain that you are not in danger by sorting out your sock drawer!

Extra tips for a good night's sleep

1. Consider going to bed earlier in order to maximise your time spent in slow-wave sleep. I know this can be difficult, so do it slowly over time. You could start your night-time routine just 15 minutes earlier and then build it up from there. Listen to your body when you start to feel tired. Avoid stifling your yawns and ploughing on. Each time you override your natural rhythms, you put extra stress on your body.

2. Try to avoid alcohol last thing at night. If you are drinking alcohol to help you sleep, be aware that once the alcohol has been broken down, sugar will be released into your system, which causes you to wake up earlier than usual.

3. Try to reduce your caffeine. As well as coffee, pay attention to the caffeine levels in energy drinks, tea and chocolate. You can store up high levels of caffeine throughout the day without realising. If you feel you are immune to the stimulating effects of coffee, it is important to note that it can prevent you from entering a deep sleep so avoid it late at night if you can.

4. Your body temperature needs to drop slightly in order to fall asleep and this explains why trying to fall asleep in an overly warm environment can be difficult. A hot bath can be helpful before going to bed because afterwards the body naturally cools itself down. Sometimes turning the pillow

or the covers to get the cooler side can also help if you wake up in the night.

5. Make sure exercise is over two hours before bedtime, otherwise your adrenalin is high and it can take a long time for the mind and body to calm down and relax.

6. Try having a small carbohydrate snack before you go to bed, such as some bread and warm milk. This will encourage the release of serotonin, which helps to induce sleep.

7. Use thick curtains or blackout blinds. A dark room encourages melatonin, which promotes sleep.

8. If you can, avoid sleeping in during the day because it upsets your natural cycle.

9. Exposure to sunlight in the morning will help you sleep at night because it helps to activate your sleep-wake cycle. The sooner you wake up and get outside, the earlier you will be able to fall asleep at night.

The importance of exercise

Dr Candace Pert discovered that opiate receptors (feel-good receptors) were not just in the brain but in every cell in the body.[19] This means that when happy chemical messengers are sent out, the effect is felt everywhere and the message spreads from cell to cell like a wave of pleasure. These pleasure waves are activated when we do physical exercise. The reason we're told so many times that exercise is so good for our mental health is because it really is.

Research shows that regular exercise is one of the best remedies for anxiety.[20]

- It releases feel-good chemicals. This helps to change our mood

- When we feel anxious, we release stress hormones. When we exercise, we burn them off.

- Light to moderate intensity exercise for at least 30 minutes a day at least five days a week can help improve the function of the relaxation response. It will help you reset your stress dial and improve your ability to bounce back from stress.

- Exercise can help you get used to, and cope with, physical changes that occur in your body. In Step 1, we looked at the similarities between our natural exercise response and the symptoms we feel during a panic attack. By regularly doing exercise, you can slowly become accustomed to the sensations in your body when the sympathetic nervous system is activated. This will give you confidence in handling strong sensations when you are feeling anxious. A brisk walk or jog whilst breathing through the nose will allow you to encounter hyperventilation in a non-threatening way. You will be able to observe the sensations of your heart beating strongly or your legs shaking, and can tell yourself, 'Okay, this is just an exercise response at the wrong time and in the wrong place.' The sensations will never again have such a strong and frightening hold over you.

There are so many different ways you can enjoy exercise – you don't need to force yourself to go to the gym if you find it the worst thing to do in the world. Walking is one of the best forms of exercise. If you go for a walk in natural surroundings, you will kill two birds with one stone because being in nature also helps to reduce stress levels.

A ten-minute exercise routine that has many health benefits

Would you like to find an exercise that has tremendous health benefits and that you can do in the comfort of your home in as little as ten to 15 minutes a day? I recently came across the exercise known as rebounding (which means bouncing up and down on a trampoline) and it has totally changed my exercise regime. I feel more energised, I sleep better, but best of all I enjoy it and it doesn't take up too much of my time!

Your body is made up of about 37 trillion cells. When you bounce up into the air you are weightless, allowing all your cells to decompress and relieve tension. As you descend, your cells feel the full force of gravity and over time this impact strengthens every one of them. There are so many benefits to bouncing on a trampoline.[21] Let me tell you about one of them.

From time to time, many of us wonder how healthy our heart is and consider taking exercise to improve its function. However, very few of us (myself included) consider the health of our lymphatic system. This is your defence mechanism against infection; it removes waste and toxins from your body. Whereas our heart has a pump to move blood around the body, the lymphatic system doesn't. It relies on us moving regularly for it to function. If we don't move, the lymphatic system can't do its job and our cells are left sitting in their own waste products. When the cells are surrounded by waste they become sluggish, tired and vulnerable to illness such as degenerative diseases and cancers.

Any exercise or movement will aid your lymphatic system, but bouncing up and down on a trampoline increases your lymph flow as much as 15 times! It really is an effective way to detoxify the body. You don't need to bounce up high; low controlled bounces are all that is needed to receive the benefits. Fifteen minutes of bouncing is equivalent to a 60-minute run.[21] This alone had me hooked when I read it – you mean, I only need to do 15 minutes a day and I don't have to leave the house? Yes!

You can buy a small 40-inch indoor trampoline relatively cheaply. I highly recommend buying one with bungee ropes rather than springs, and it may also be a good idea to get one with a handle or frame to hold on to. The internet has plenty of great rebounding routines, or just put on a TV programme that you like and bounce away. I was truly amazed when I discovered all its benefits, how little time each day I needed to do it – and how much fun it was, considering it was exercise!

Some people who have a weak pelvic floor can be wary of bouncing on a trampoline. Although rebounding has been shown to strengthen and tone pelvic floor muscles,[21] it is important to seek medical advice if you are unsure if this exercise is right for you.

*I strongly advise you to consult with your doctor before you proceed with rebounding or any new form of exercise regime.

The importance of diet

The gut is extremely clever; it is known as our 'second brain'. It has millions of neurons and is in constant direct communication with the brain. Our large and small intestines are packed with messenger cells that are all exchanging information with emotional content. This is why we get a 'gut feeling' about someone or a place. It is also why we 'trust our gut' and go with it when making important decisions.

In your gut there is an army of trillions of microbes that influences mood, weight and the immune system. What you eat has a huge impact on the type of microbes that thrive. An unhealthy gut is the cause of a lot of mental and physical health issues.[22] Research has revolutionised doctors' understanding of the links between the food we eat, the way we feel, and even the way we think.[22]

We all know we should eat a healthy diet to have a healthy body, but we also need to be more aware of just how much a healthy diet can affect our mood. Some foods can strengthen your resilience to stress, whereas others can create stress and illness in your body. If you are not keen on eliminating foods from your diet that you really like, try adding more foods that are good for your mind and for your body. For example, Omega-3 fatty acids are hugely important in our diet. They have been studied thoroughly for their effects on heart health and inflammation; more recently, they have been shown to have a beneficial impact on mental health and are now recommended to help treat some forms of depression and anxiety.[23]

Food allergies cause inflammation in the body, which can cause mood disorders. If you have any physical symptoms such as headaches, inflammation or digestive issues, it might be a good idea to get a food allergy test to see if what you are eating may be causing the problem. It is possible to suffer from a food allergy and not be aware of it. Many people suffering from anxiety and depression are now consulting dieticians as scientists are becoming increasingly aware of the links between what we are eating and how we are feeling.

If you feel this information applies to you, consider talking to a doctor or dietician to learn more about which diet is best for you.

Healthy ways to keep your nervous system flexible

When we feel we are drowning in fear and anxiety, we can turn to unhealthy habits to calm ourselves down such as alcohol, drugs, self-harming behaviours or compulsive rituals. I want to give you a list of some healthy activities that you can participate in regularly. In conjunction with the audios, these will continue to flex your nervous system and prevent you from becoming overwhelmed.

Singing

Making sounds with your voice, whether humming, chanting or singing, changes the vibration of your nervous system. Singing, in particular, has a calming yet energising effect on your nervous system. It releases endorphins and reduces stress and anxiety, brings balance and control to your breathing, and gives your nervous system a workout.

After learning about singing and its positive effects, I wasn't sure what to do. Joining a choir or forming a band were not an option for me because I can't carry a tune to save my life! I knew many of my clients would be in the same position, so I decided to find another way to feel all the benefits of singing without damaging the eardrums of those around me.

If, like me, you can't hold a tune or don't have time to join a choir, find a place where you won't be disturbed – or, more importantly, where you won't disturb anyone else. Your car is a good place. Lock the door, put on some headphones, choose a powerful rock song and belt out every word at the top of your voice. Not only will this release happy chemicals and make you feel good, it will also give your nervous system a workout. Have a short playlist; depending on time, you can do one or a few songs. I recommend doing this at least once a day. I don't advise doing it whilst driving as you need to give the song your full attention. If you are having difficulty choosing a song, I can recommend 'You shook me all night long' by AC/DC!

Although it sounds straightforward, there is an exact science to this. I have written the steps for you to follow below. Don't laugh before you've tried it!

1. Park the car. You need your full commitment!

2. Put on your headphones. Select 'You shook me all night long' or your chosen power song and turn up the volume. Then turn it up some more!

3. As the beat comes in, feel it go straight to your heartbeat and notice how it connects with and vibrates in every cell in your body.

4. Don't underestimate how much movement can be achieved whilst sitting in your car. Start to move your hips by clenching the right buttock and then the left buttock. After a while, they will continue on their own!

5. Start to sway and move your head from side to side to the beat.

6. Notice the excitement in the body as it begins to realise the chorus is coming up.

7. Let rip and sing out every word of the chorus. Go hard, or go home!

8. Lift your arms and fist bump the air.

9. Air-guitar action during the guitar solo is optional.

10. Repeat as many times as needed.

Joking aside, this really is an effective way to stimulate and flex your nervous system. Your heart pounds and adrenalin is released. Sensations that you would normally fear are now interpreted as excitement. If no one is in the house and the neighbours are out, it is even better to do this whilst dancing and moving your whole body. That would also allow you to fall to your knees for the air-guitar solo!

Music has the power to evoke emotional responses. Adding chilling music in a horror film or arousing music in an action film dramatically adds to our experience whilst watching it. Listening to music that we love releases happy chemicals, fast-paced music increases our arousal, and music with a slow tempo relaxes us. Create your own playlist that moves you up and down and flexes your nervous system.

Music can instantly change how we feel. If you begin to notice some anxiety in your body whilst at work or at a social gathering, turn to whoever you are with and say, 'I'll be right back, I just need to get something from my car!'

Join a drumming circle

Creating music is also therapeutic for the nervous system. An instrument that has been shown throughout history to be healing is the drum. The rhythm we connect to is tribal and instinctual, and it calms the tension in our body. Drumming is expressive and cathartic, and is being used more and more in helping people with trauma and anxiety.[24]

If, like me, you are not very musical and don't have space for a drum kit, don't panic. You can easily buy a cheap djembe drum and join a drumming circle. There are lots of free lessons on the internet to learn a few simple rhythms to build your confidence before you go, but you really don't need to be skilled. Banging on your drum whilst listening to the beats of the other drums in the circle is truly an amazing feeling that I can't recommend enough. Not only does it feel good, it also reduces the release of stress hormones. Drumming eases tension whilst energising your nervous system. Being part of a drumming circle will also introduce you to a new community of people.

Focus the mind

Yoga is well known for focussing the mind and the breath, and for releasing tension from the body. If yoga is not your thing, consider other practices that can also improve your mental and physical health by integrating posture, movement, breathing techniques and focussed intent.

I recommend looking into Qigong and also the self-defence martial art Aikido. These practices allow you to gain much deeper insights into how you feel and how you think, which in turn will make the audios and techniques easier.

Laugh

A good hearty laugh relieves physical tension and stress in the body. Laughing is the ideal antidote to anxiety; it stimulates your nervous system in a positive way and it boosts your immune system. There are many comedy clubs around, but if you prefer to stay at home, find clips on the internet of comedians that you like or sketches from films that make you laugh. Make an effort to watch something that makes you laugh at least once a day. This is a great way to help your body rest and restore because your muscles remain relaxed for up to 45 minutes after having a good laugh.

Step 5 takeaways

1. Slow-wave sleep is extremely important for restoring and replenishing the cells and tissues in your body and for boosting your immune system.

2. Dream sleep (or REM sleep) destresses your arousals from the day. The more arousals you have, the more dream sleep you need. Dream sleep is not restful sleep; when you spend more than two hours in dream sleep you can feel more tired than you did before going to bed.

3. Resting and restoring the mind and body during the day improves the quality of your sleep.

4. Try using the bonus sleeping audio to retrain your brain to fall asleep naturally.

5. If you lie in bed with your mind racing, the adrenalin in your system and the high frequency of your brain waves will prevent you from sleeping. Get up and find a boring activity that will calm the brain. When you feel tired, go back to bed and try to sleep again.

6. Exercise has many benefits for both your physical and mental health.

7. Consider what kind of foods you are eating and how healthy they are for your gut. The gut is known as 'the second brain'; there is now lots of evidence that shows strong links between our diet and our mood.

8. Try a new activity to keep your nervous system flexible, such as singing or joining a drumming circle.

What's the next step?

Choosing your next step

Some people may feel motivated after reading a self-help book but fail to take action because they are not sure where to start and need guidance. One of the reasons for including audios in this book is to enable you to start your journey as soon as you put this book down.

Your plan to reset your stress dial will be unique to you. You already know instinctively when you need to have a drink or eat something or take a nap. Start to tune in to how stressed you feel and when your stress is at its highest. This is the time to close your eyes and stimulate your relaxation response. Close your eyes for five minutes, count your breaths or do a body scan. Taking five minutes to rest and restore the body a few times a day is a great start to resetting your stress dial.

It is also important to take the time to relax your mind and body deeply, so look at your schedule and decide when in the day you can fit in a 25-minute guided relaxation. For the first three weeks at least, you need to try to commit to one of the longer audios once if not twice a day in order to create new pathways in the brain.

The recordings and exercises will enable you to become more aware of your physical experience. You can begin to accept your sensations and learn to let them go instead of being fearful of them. Rather than being at war with your body, you will become its ally. When your body is anxious and calls you up to let you know, pick up the phone! You need to listen to what your body is telling you. The phone will keep ringing until you do. Avoid arguing with it, just listen, observe and be understanding. Show the body that there is no danger by stimulating the relaxation response with the techniques mentioned in Steps 1, 2 and 3. Once you feel calmer, slow your thoughts down and change your focus using the exercises from Step 4.

Use scaling to measure your progress

Build up your resilience to stress step by step. Make notes and use scales to notice how you are feeling from one day to the next. This is very important because sometimes it can be difficult to really see how far you have come and so you can lose your motivation. When people lose weight, they can use weighing scales or a tape measure to record how much they have lost. You can't measure your anxiety with a tape measure – but you can use scales. Before using an audio or a technique in the book, write down on a scale from 1 to 10 how you are feeling, 10 being the most anxious you can feel and 1 being no anxiety at all.

Monitor how intense your anxiety attacks feel after using the techniques and audios on your scale. Even if the number comes down only one notch at first, this is a win to celebrate. Be aware that it is possible to have a string of really good days where you record low numbers on your scale and then there is a day when your anxiety is back at a 9. That's okay; this process is not a straight line. Expect to go up and down. Instead of feeling frustrated, be curious about why it was high on a particular day and learn from what happened. Use the visualisation technique to imagine how you would handle the situation better next time. By staying curious, in control and committed to the process, you will continue to build your strength and resilience to stress on good and bad days.

Scaling is also a good way to break down all-or-nothing thinking. When the emotional brain takes over and says 'I'm anxious all the time', or 'I never feel relaxed', use your scale to test how true these statements are. If you have a bad day and think, 'My goodness, my anxiety is a 10 today,' it means that there are days when it is not so high. If it is a 7, ask yourself what you could do to make it come down to a 6. If your anxiety is at a 6, ask yourself what stops it being a 7 or an 8. Using a scale is very useful because it allows you to monitor your bodily sensations very closely, and by observing your physical experience you are more likely to keep the thinking brain engaged for longer. You may want to start a journal to log and review your progress, and to note positive changes you notice and any areas that need more attention.

Making changes to the way you feel and the way you think is a process. Try not to overestimate how much you will change in a day – but don't underestimate how much you can change in a couple of weeks. Have compassion for yourself. Imagine someone you loved read this book and asked for your support. If they failed to follow the steps for a couple of days, or had a bad day where they still felt highly anxious and forgot the steps, would you be angry and frustrated with them? No, you would encourage them and tell them to learn from their setbacks and to celebrate their wins.

Why can it be difficult to adopt new ideas and behaviours?

Have you ever been to a self-development workshop and felt inspired and motivated to make changes in your life as soon as you got home but these changes never happened? I once went to a workshop on the benefits of getting up at 5am. As I listened to the woman speak of the benefits of joining the five o'clock club, such as getting three hours of work in before breakfast, I thought it sounded a great idea. I was definitely going to join the other people around the world who got up at this hour. I made a list of all the things I was going to do between 5am and 8am.

I got home from the workshop all fired up and excited about my new routine. I set my alarm before getting into bed and then, when the morning came and my alarm went off, I opened one eye, groaned, pressed the snooze button and turned over. When I finally woke up and had my breakfast at 8.30 with the rest of the world, I felt really cross with myself. Why, when I really wanted to do it and told myself I was going to do it, did I *not* do it?

The simple answer is that my unconscious mind saw more pain than pleasure in getting up so early. We are ruled by these two basic emotions; we move away from pain and towards pleasure. I woke up, I felt tired, it was cold outside and my bedclothes were warm and soft; my unconscious mind saw a lot of unnecessary effort and pain in getting up, and it resisted. When I felt that I should at least try to get up, my mind supplied me with excuses why I didn't need to. It said, 'But you're so tired and you worked so hard yesterday. It's nice to stay in bed and I'm sure you can work twice as hard after breakfast to make up the time.' I agreed with the excuses and went back to sleep.

This may sound familiar if you have had difficulty changing an old habit. You can try all you like but until your unconscious mind sees more pain than pleasure in your changes then forget it. We saw earlier that the conscious mind has only 5% control whereas the unconscious mind has 95%. Many of us may consciously decide to lose weight and go on a healthy diet, but if unconsciously we see pain in doing this, we won't keep it up for long.

It's not 'where there's a will, there's a way' because, when it comes down to it, our will is pretty weak. It is more about where there is pain there is a way! Once you see more pain than pleasure in continuing bad habits, change can happen in an instant.

We can change our habits overnight; all we need is a breakthrough moment where we say, 'I'm done, no more.' You suddenly see more pain in staying as you are than in changing. For example, a person who used to smoke 40 cigarettes a day, had a fried breakfast every morning and wouldn't dream of changing their ways suffers a near-fatal heart attack. The next day the cigarettes have gone, muesli is now on the menu for breakfast and they are taking regular walks around the park. A week before their heart attack they would have sworn blind that it wasn't possible to squeeze a 20-minute walk into their busy schedule but now they have a strong motivation to change. Change really can happen that fast; it doesn't have to take years.

You may read this book and feel motivated to take action, but after a week or two you still haven't scheduled in the time to listen to an audio or try a technique. Avoid waiting until you are facing major pain, such as ill health, before you start to make changes.

To help yourself commit to using these five steps, ask yourself why you want to free yourself from anxiety.

What is your reason for wanting to reset your stress dial?

You may think the answer is obvious – 'I don't want to feel anxious all the time' – but it might not be a strong enough reason for you to take long-term action. The only way you will commit to making changes in your life is if you have a deep and meaningful reason.

The first time I met Jack, I sent him home with a relaxation audio. When he came to see me the following week, I asked him how many times he'd listened to it. He looked a little sheepish and said, 'Only once, but I haven't had much time this week.'

I told him that if he had a strong enough reason to make changes in his life, he would be surprised at how possible it was to find the time. I asked him why he wanted to be in control of his anxiety. He looked at me as if I were mad because obviously he didn't enjoy feeling anxious.

Many of us would like to be thinner because we don't like how we feel, or we would like to give up an addiction because we don't like what it is doing to our bodies, but how many of us commit to making changes that would help us lose the weight quickly or put our addiction to one side? The only way to do this is to go deeper than your surface reason for changing.

I continued to dig deeper with Jack and asked him why he didn't want to feel anxious. He said he didn't like who he was when he was fearful. I asked why he didn't like himself when he was fearful. Every time he gave me an answer, I asked, 'And why is that?' Finally, on the sixth or seventh time of asking, he shouted at me, 'Because I don't want to lose my girlfriend.'

His emotion and his admission surprised him. He looked at me and said, 'Yeah, I guess deep down I'm frightened she will leave me if I don't sort myself out.' I told him to remind himself of this reason every time he came up with an excuse not to take 25 minutes in the day for himself to relax his nervous system. Once he had the 'why', unsurprisingly he was able to find the time.

This approach of finding your 'why' is based on Joe Stump's Seven Levels Deep exercise.[25] It is an effective technique to find your motivation and drive. Try to do this for yourself using the exercise template below. Every answer you give will be used as the next question. For example:

Why do you want to be in control of your anxiety?

Because I don't like feeling anxious.

Why don't you like feeling anxious?

Because I don't like who I am when I am fearful.

Why don't you like who you are when you are fearful?

...etc

Continue in this way for seven questions and see if you can uncover a deeper and stronger reason to make changes in your life.

Seven Levels Deep questionnaire

Why do you want to be in control of your anxiety?	Because...
Why...	Because...
Why...	Because...
Why...	Because...
Why...	Because...

Why...	Because...
Why...	Because...

Watch out for your unconscious mind!

Despite having good intentions and your reason 'why', your unconscious mind may continue to get in the way sometimes. It is important to prepare yourself for the arguments it will make as you start this journey of change. The unconscious mind is stuck in its ways; you therefore need to make a stand again and again so that you don't get pushed around or dictated to. Continue to remind yourself of your 'why', and continue to ignore the unconscious mind. It will get on board with the plan once your new changes have become your new habits.

Let's look at some of the thoughts and questions that may try to creep in and thwart your progress.

I can't take this time for myself; I have people that depend on me.

If you have travelled on an airplane, you will know that when the air steward gives you the safety and emergency demonstration, they tell you to put your oxygen mask on first before helping anyone else. You may think the best thing to do is to help your loved one first, but they need you to be fit and well, not just to put their mask on. You need to be at your best physically and mentally for your family, so rather than seeing taking this time for yourself as selfish, see it as a priority.

Once you are familiar with the techniques in this book, you can teach them to your loved ones. Anxiety in children and teenagers is on the rise. Teaching them what is going on in their bodies and how to take back control is a great way to build their resilience at an early age. You can encourage them to create their own play list and to get involved in activities that calm and flex the nervous system, such as singing, drumming, yoga or aikido. I had one client who prepared a power song for all the family to sing at the top of their voices before and after school. She swears by it and says it sets them all up for the day.

I'm feeling better. I'm sure I can go back to full speed ahead again.

If someone lost lots of weight because they had started to eat healthily and go to the gym regularly, it would be a waste of their good work to then decide to go back to sitting on the couch eating takeaways. The same principle applies to these new changes you are about to make. You need to repeat these behaviours regularly to make long-term and permanent change. The fact that you are feeling better is a sign that it is working and your stress dial has reset. You want to keep it this way. Most people who commit to eating healthily find it becomes not only easy but natural; new habits have formed and the thought of eating greasy foods becomes unappealing. I have found the same thing in myself and my clients with building up resilience to stress. You start to feel so much calmer and in control of your anxiety that you can't imagine going back to your old habits and lifestyle because you fear feeling the way you did before.

I don't think it will work for me.

Maybe some of you are thinking, 'I'm sure this has worked for other people, but my mind and body are so stuck in their ways that it just won't work for me.' If these thoughts come in, remind yourself that the human brain is beyond amazing.

The brain contains 100 billion neurons; scientists have called it 'the most complex object in the known universe'. Despite all the recent advances in cognitive science and the neurosciences, there is still so much about it that we don't know. It just isn't possible to say that we know our own brains well and understand what they can and can't do.

We read stories all the time about people who have suffered damage to one part of their brain and been told they will never speak again. Then, over time, a different part of their brain takes over this function and they do learn to speak again. It takes time and effort but the brain is neuroplastic; it can learn new things, adapt and – most importantly – change.

Your brain really can take on new behaviours, habits and ways of thinking. It can learn to let go of unwanted thoughts and replace them with loving thoughts, and it can learn to bounce back from stress and keep calm instead of stimulating your fight-or-flight response.

Are you sure there isn't a quick fix?

A man saw an advertisement that said, 'If you want big muscles, order our muscle kit today.' He made the order. When he received the manual through the post, he phoned the company and said, 'Thank you, I have just received my manual. Could you tell me when you'll be sending the muscles?'

If you think that your life is too hectic and it isn't possible to squeeze in five minutes to breathe, let alone 25 minutes to relax deeply, you are a number one candidate for bringing these five steps into your life!

No one is immune from major and minor stressors in their life. However, the more you overcome your problems, the stronger your resilience grows. By flexing your resilience muscle again and again, it will get stronger. The more you work on resetting your nervous system every day, and the more you work on handling difficult thoughts, the more able you will be to deal with what comes your way. That may not seem true or possible right now, but wait and see how you change over the next few weeks and months whilst using these techniques and audios.

You will grow in resilience and confidence every time you solve and face a new problem whilst keeping your anxiety at bay. Don't forget that you will never eradicate stress or anxiety; you can only change how your mind and body respond to it. The bigger the problem you solve, the more powerful you will feel. Problems and difficult stressors will always be there but it is how you cope that shows you how strong you really are.

The next step takeaways

1. Start to listen more closely to your body during the day to know when to rest and restore for a few minutes.

2. Schedule in your 25-minute guided relaxation once a day, or twice if you can.

3. Use a scale to track your progress. If your anxiety is a 6 right now, what could you do to reduce it to 5? If it is a 9, what stops it being a 10? Become more familiar with your physical sensations by observing them.

4. We are motivated to make changes when we see more pain than pleasure in staying as we are.

5. Find your real reason for making changes. Once you have a strong enough 'why', you will take positive action.

6. Watch out for the excuses your unconscious mind will come up with to avoid making changes.

Conclusion

***What progress, you ask, have I made? I have begun to be
a friend to myself.*** - Hecato

Once Jack had found his motivation, there was no stopping
him. After seven weeks of sessions together, he was well
on his way to getting his life back on track. He returned to
work and started playing football again at the weekends. He
was socialising more in the evenings and had booked a long
weekend in New York for himself and his girlfriend.

I asked him how he felt when he was at work or out with
friends. He told me that sometimes he felt a little anxious
before he left the house but the feeling didn't linger. He said
that he couldn't explain why but he felt something inside
him had shifted and he was no longer a prisoner in his own
body. Not only had he not had another panic attack, he no
longer feared them. He said he felt confident in his ability
to take back control whenever he felt symptoms of anxiety
start to bubble up. Instead of giving his anxiety a name, he
chose to visualise it as his own personal guard dog. When
the dog started barking for no reason, he smiled at it and
told it to quieten down because everything was fine. As
soon as he had a mental image of this nervous dog taking
its cue from its master, he felt the sensations that had arisen
slowly fade away.

This new sense of control had built up his confidence and allowed him to go back to work and book a holiday because he knew he had the final say, even if his dog started barking. He felt powerful because he had experienced again and again how his body responded when he rehearsed stimulating the relaxation response. He no longer felt angry towards his body because he understood it was just barking and growling to protect him, and it was up to him to reassure his body that there was no immediate threat. By making friends with his anxiety, he had created peace in his body.

The changes he had made had a knock-on effect in other areas in his life. He was less irritable in general and could resolve arguments with his girlfriend calmly, whereas before he had often felt overwhelmed and would simply shut down. He could now talk about his mother and recall happy memories of her before she died, memories that he hadn't been able to go near for a very long time.

Is Jack's life now perfect? Not at all. Does he still have problems and feel stressed? Of course he does, but he can face these challenges. His anxiety is no longer given the chance to escalate because he understands what is going on and why. Instead of being angry at his body, he now reassures it that there is no danger present. By continuing to make the effort to look after himself, he manages to keep his stress dial low. Every time he bounces back from the stresses in his life, the more confident and resilient he feels.

We all face stressors and major challenges in our lives. In order to overcome them, we need to have a healthy nervous system. If your dial is turned up high, even the little problems in life can push you over the edge.

The aim of this book is not to eliminate your anxiety; it is not possible to get rid of this ancient survival response that evolved to protect you. You wouldn't last two minutes in this world without it. Remember that it is nature's gift to you, your ally, not your enemy.

My hope is that in time you will begin to make friends with your body and start to listen to what it is trying to tell you. Anxiety is the way we express stress. If you continue to push your body or ignore and hide from its messages, it has no choice but to start screaming at you to get your attention. It isn't screaming to hurt you but because it so desperately needs you to listen to what is happening inside you. It is either trying to tell you to slow down, to rest and restore because it can't keep up with the stress and pace of your life, or it is trying to tell you that there is some trauma in the nervous system that needs to be resolved and processed. Or it might be trying to tell you that you are not meeting your emotional needs. The longer you ignore these messages or silence them, the louder they will get.

Suffering from anxiety is like being held prisoner in your own body and it can take courage to take back control. The first step is the hardest, but you have already taken five steps by reading this book. Use these five steps again and again to support and guide you on your journey. They will help you break free from the chains of anxiety, not by waging a war with your body but by becoming a good friend to yourself.

If you have found this book helpful and would like to leave a review on Amazon so that others can benefit from it too, I would be very grateful. Otherwise, until we meet again, I wish you all the best.

Vivienne

Freedom from Anxiety in Five Steps

About the Author

Vivienne Emery (MA, BSc, Dip. Psychotherapy) is a psychotherapist, author and coach. She currently runs her own therapy clinic in the south-east of England. Her free e-books on depression and PTSD are circulated by local charities and in GP surgeries to help people in severe distress make changes in the way they perceive and understand their symptoms.

For more information on Vivienne Emery and her books, courses and training go to

www.vivienneemery.com

References

1 LeDoux, J (1998) *The Emotional Brain.* Weidenfeld & Nicolson

2 Goleman, D (1996) *Emotional Intelligence.* Bloomsbury

3 Porges, S (1995) 'Orienting in a defensive world: Mammalian modifications of our evolutionary heritage. A Polyvagal Theory'. *Psychophysiology* 32:301-318.

4 Porges, S, Dana, D (2018) *Clinical Applications of the Polyvagal Theory: The emergence of Polyvagal-informed Therapies.* W.W. Norton & Company Ltd.

5 Dana, D (2018) *The Polyvagal Theory in Therapy.* W.W. Norton & Company Ltd.

6a Griffin, J, Tyrrell, I (2003) *A New Approach to Emotional Health and Clear Thinking.* HG Publishing, East Sussex.

6b Murphy, M. (2007). Testing treatment for trauma. Human Givens, 14 (4), 37-42.

7 Griffin, J, Tyrrell, I (2005*) Freedom From Addiction: The secret behind successful addiction busting.* HG Publishing, East Sussex.

8 Ryan, R, Edward, L. Deci (2018) *Self-Determination Theory: Basic Psychological Needs in Motivation, Development, and Wellness***.** Guilford Press

9a https://www.livescience.com/21778-early-neglect-alters-kids-brains.html

9b http://www.digma.com/digma-images/video-scripts/fredericks_experiment.pdf

*10*https://www.medicalnewstoday.com/articles/318723#Loneliness

11 https://www.holmleigh-care.co.uk/link-social-media-anxiety-mental-health

12 https://www.anxietyuk.org.uk/blog/covid-19-and-anxiety

13 Girodo, J, 'Yoga meditation and flooding in the treatment of anxiety neurosis', Journal of Behaviour Therapy and Experimental Psychiatry., 5 (2):157-160.

14 https://deltadiscoverycenter.com/effects-yoga-nidra-stress-anxiety-overall-wellness/

15 Miller, R (2015) *The iRest Program for Healing PTSD.* New Harbinger Publications, Inc

16 Lipton, B, (2008) *The Biology of Belief: Unleashing the power of consciousness, matter and miracles.* Hay House UK Ltd

17 Atkinson, W (2010) *The Law of Attraction and How to Master This Great Power.* Kessinger Publishing

18 Griffin, J, and Tyrrel, I (2004) *Dreaming Reality: How dreaming keeps us sane, or can drive us mad.* HG Publishing, East Sussex.

19 Pert, C. (1999) *Molecules of Emotion.* Simon & Schuster UK

*20*https://www.ncbi.nlm.nih.gov/pmc/articles/PMC3632802/

21 https://www.fitnessguides.co.uk/benefits-of-rebounding/

22 https://www.health.harvard.edu/blog/gut-feelings-how-food-affects-your-mood

23 https//www.psychologytoday.com/us/blog/in-th-zone/anxiety-and-omega-3-fatty-acids

24 https://www.rhythmresearchresources.net/research-drum-therapy-introduction

25 https://digitalbloggers.com/business/Discover-Your-Why-Seven-Levels-Deep

DISCLAIMER

Last updated: 01/08/2020

The information provided in *Freedom from Anxiety in Five Steps* and the resources available for download are for educational and general informational purposes only and it is not intended as, and shall not be understood or construed as, professional medical advice, diagnosis, or treatment, or substitute for professional medical advice, diagnosis, or treatment.

Before taking any actions based upon such information, we expressly recommend that you seek advice from a medical professional.

Your use of this book, including implementation of any suggestions and/or recommendations set out in it and/or use of any resources available for download through the site, does not create a doctor–patient relationship.

Your use of this book is solely at your own risk and you expressly agree not to rely upon any information contained in the book or in the resources available for download through the Site as a substitute for professional medical advice, diagnosis, or treatment.

Under no circumstance shall the author be held liable or responsible for any errors or omissions in the book or for any damage you may suffer in respect to any actions taken or not taken based on any or all of the contents of the book and/or as a result of failing to seek competent advice from a medical professional.

All information in the book is provided in good faith and every reasonable effort has been made to ensure that the information provided is as accurate and complete as possible and free from errors; however, the author assumes no responsibility for errors, omissions, or contrary interpretation, and make no representation or warranty of any kind, express or implied, regarding the accuracy, adequacy, relevance, validity, reliability, availability, timeliness or completeness of any information in the book.

Under no circumstance shall the author be held liable for any special, direct, indirect, consequential, or incidental loss or damage or any damages of any kind incurred as a result of the use of the book reliance on any information provided in the book.

By using the book, you accept full personal responsibility for any harm or damage you suffer as a result of your actions arising out of or in connection with the use of the book or its content.

You agree to use judgment and conduct due diligence to verify any information obtained from the book before taking any action or implementing any suggestions or recommendations set out in the book.

Your use of the book is solely at your own risk and you expressly agree not to rely upon any information contained in the book.

We reserve the right to make additions, deletions, or modification to the contents on the book at any time without prior notice.

We do not warrant that the Site used is free of viruses or other harmful components. Any perceived slights of specific persons, peoples, or organizations are unintentional.

Any product, website, and company names mentioned in the book are the trademarks or copyright properties of their respective owners. We are not affiliated with them in any way.

The book may contain links to external websites that are not provided or maintained by or in any way affiliated with us. The author does not guarantee the accuracy, adequacy, relevance, validity, reliability, availability, timeliness or completeness of any information on these external websites.

Printed in Great Britain
by Amazon